Landmarks of world literature

Gustave Flaubert

MADAME BOVARY

Landmarks of world literature

General Editor: J. P. Stern

GUSTAVE FLAUBERT

Madame Bovary

STEPHEN HEATH

*Professor of the History of Consciousness, University of
California, Santa Cruz and Fellow of Jesus College, Cambridge*

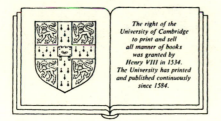

The right of the
University of Cambridge
to print and sell
all manner of books
was granted by
Henry VIII in 1534.
The University has printed
and published continuously
since 1584.

CAMBRIDGE UNIVERSITY PRESS

Cambridge
New York   Port Chester
Melbourne   Sydney

Published by the Press Syndicate of the University of Cambridge
The Pitt Building, Trumpington Street, Cambridge CB2 1RP
40 West 20th Street, New York, NY 10011-4211, USA
10 Stamford Road, Oakleigh, Victoria 3166, Australia

© Cambridge University Press 1992

First published 1992

Printed in Great Britain at the University Press, Cambridge

A catalogue record for this book is available from the British Library

Library of Congress cataloguing in publication data

Heath, Stephen.
Gustave Flaubert, Madame Bovary / Stephen Heath.
     p.   cm. – (Landmarks of world literature)
Includes bibliographical references.
ISBN 0 521 32805 5. – ISBN 0 521 31483 6 (paperback)
1. Flaubert, Gustave, 1821–1880. Madame Bovary. I. Title.
II. Series.
PQ2246. M3H38   1992   91–19758
843'.8 – dc20   CIP

ISBN 0 521 32805 5 hardback
ISBN 0 521 31483 6 paperback

**Transferred to
Digital Reprinting 1999**

**Printed in the
United States of America**

GG

'Le but? le but? le sens? qui le sait?'
Flaubert, *Par les champs et par les grèves*, 1847
(*OC* II, 484)

Contents

Note on references

References to *Madame Bovary* are to part and chapter numbers and are given in brackets after quotations (e.g. II,7). The text used is that of the Classiques Garnier edition by Claudine Gothot-Mersch, Paris, Garnier, 1971. Translations are largely my own, though the available English versions have been consulted and their renderings used where appropriate; details of these versions can be found in the Guide to further reading.

Quotations from other works by Flaubert, as from the speeches and judgement at the trial of *Madame Bovary*, are from *Œuvres complètes*, 2 volumes, Collection l'Intégrale, Paris, Seuil, 1964, abbreviated *OC* with references given to volume and page numbers (e.g. *OC* I, 302). Exceptions are quotations from (i) *Dictionnaire des idées reçues*, references to which are to the Folio edition of *Bouvard et Pécuchet* by Claudine Gothot-Mersch, Paris, Gallimard, 1979 (the most complete and methodical edition available, including a number of 'idées' not in *OC*), abbreviated *BP* and accompanied by the page number (e.g. *BP*, 341); (ii) the notebook kept by Flaubert from c.1838–41 entitled (by his niece) *Souvenirs, notes et pensées intimes*, where references are to the edition by J. P. Germain, Paris, A.-G. Nizet, 1987, abbreviated *SNPI* with the page number following (e.g. *SNPI*, 26); (iii) the draft material for *Madame Bovary* published, with initial plans, scenarios and sketches, as *Madame Bovary, nouvelle version précédée des scénarios inédits*, edited by Jean Pommier and Gabrielle Leleu, Paris, José Corti, 1949, references being given to the page number after the abbreviation *NV* (e.g. *NV*, 103).

References to Flaubert's letters are made by date and correspondent, using initials for the latter as follows: C – Louise Colet; B – Louis Bouilhet (these two are the recipients of the majority of the letters quoted here); EC – Ernest Chevalier; MDC – Maxime Du Camp; JD – Jules Duplan; EF – Ernest Feydeau; ALP – Alfred Le Poittevin; LdC – Marie-Sophie Leroyer de Chantepie; RdG – Edma Roger des Genettes; GS – George Sand (thus '23 December 1853, C' means a letter of that date to Louise Colet; 'April 1857 EF', a letter to Ernest Feydeau of that month and year, day unknown; and so on); other correspondents are indicated by name on the one or two occasions each occurs; in cases where the context already clearly identifies the correspondent no initial or name is given. The source for most of the quotations is the edition of the *Correspondance* by Jean Bruneau, the three volumes of which so far published cover the years 1830–68, Bibliothèque de la Pléiade, Paris, Gallimard, 1973, 1980 and 1991; for later letters the edition used is *Œuvres complètes de Gustave Flaubert*, Paris, Club de l'Honnête Homme, 1971–5, volumes XII–XVI. Wherever possible translations are based on the small selection of the letters translated by Francis Steegmuller, *The Letters of Gustave Flaubert*, 2 volumes, Cambridge, Mass., Harvard University Press, and London, Faber, 1980 and 1982.

Information regarding other works mentioned in the text is given, where appropriate, in the Guide to further reading.

Chronology

	Flaubert's life and works	Literary events	Historical events
1821	12 December: born in the Hôtel–Dieu, Rouen, where his father is surgeon-in-chief; there is an elder brother, Achille aged eight	Hegel, *Philosophy of Right*	Death of Napoleon
1822		Hugo, *Odes et poésies diverses*	
1823		Stendhal, *Racine et Shakespeare* Scott, *Quentin Durward*	
1824	Birth of sister, Caroline	Death of Byron at Missolonghi	Death of Louis XVIII, succeeded by Charles X; power of the clerical party ('ultras'), refusal of political reform
1826		Vigny, *Poèmes antiques et modernes*; *Cinq-Mars* Cooper, *The Last of the Mohicans*	
1827		Hugo, *Cromwell*	

1829		Balzac, *Le Dernier Chouan*, *Physiologie du mariage* Hugo, *Les Orientales*	Stephenson's *Rocket*
1830		Hugo, *Hernani* Lamartine, *Harmonies poétiques et religieuses* Stendhal, *Le Rouge et le Noir*	Capture of Algiers, start of French colonial presence in Algeria July Revolution against reactionary and authoritarian regime; abdication of Charles, succeeded by Louis-Philippe, 'the bourgeois king'; power of the constitutional party, industry and finance
1830–48			July Monarchy
1831		Hugo, *Notre-Dame de Paris*	
1832	Begins school in Rouen at the Collège Royal	Balzac, *Louis Lambert* Vigny, *Stello* Beginning of the satirical paper *Le Charivari*; Daumier imprisoned for caricature of Louis-Philippe Goethe, *Faust II*	First Reform Act (England)
1833		Balzac, *Le Médecin de campagne*; *Eugénie Grandet* Sand, *Lélia*	

	Flaubert's life and works	Literary events	Historical events
1834	Start of friendship with Louis Bouilhet; beginning of period of intense early literary activity	Balzac, *Le Père Goriot* Musset, *Lorenzaccio* Sainte-Beuve, *Volupté*	Repression of worker insurrections in Lyon and Paris Poor Law Reform Act (England)
1835		Lamartine, *Voyage en Orient* Vigny, *Chatterton* Büchner, *Danton's Death*	Attempt by Fieschi on Louis-Philippe's life; increasingly repressive laws against right of association and freedom of Press
1836	On holiday at Trouville, falls in love with Elisa Foucault, twenty-five, companion and soon wife of Maurice Schlesinger: the 'only true passion' of his life, image of the loved but inaccessible woman	Gautier, *Mademoiselle de Maupin* Musset, *La Confession d'un enfant du siècle* Dickens, *Pickwick Papers*	
1837	Publication of two stories in local literary journal; writes *Passion et vertu*, a premonition of *Madame Bovary*	Balzac, *Illusions perdues* (Part I) Carlyle, *The French Revolution* Dickens, *Oliver Twist*	
1837–1901			Reign of Queen Victoria
1838	*Mémoires d'un fou*, an auto-biographical narrative dedicated to his friend Alfred Le Poittevin		Beginnings of Chartist movement in England First daguerrotypes

1839	*Smarh*, an 'old mystery', pre-figuring *La Tentation de saint Antoine*	Stendhal, *La Chartreuse de Parme*	Insurrection in Paris, Barbès and Blanqui arrested
1840	Passes *baccalauréat* examination; travels in Corsica	Proudhon, *Qu'est-ce que la propriété?*	
1841		Michelet, *Jeanne d'Arc* Feuerbach, *The Essence of Christianity*	
1842	*Novembre*, another autobiographical narrative; lives in Paris and passes first law examination	Balzac, 'Avant-Propos' to *La Comédie humaine* Sue, *Les Mystères de Paris* Gogol, *Dead Souls*	
1843	Begins first version of *L'Education sentimentale*; meets Maxime Du Camp; fails second law examination	Balzac, completion of *Illusions perdues* Hugo, *Les Burgraves* Ruskin, *Modern Painters* (first volume)	Opening of Paris–Rouen railway
1844	Has first seizure while driving a carriage at night with his brother near Pont-l'Evêque; abandons his studies and retires to the house bought by his father at Croisset, near Rouen	Dumas, *Les Trois Mousquetaires*; *Le Comte de Monte-Cristo*	

	Flaubert's life and works	Literary events	Historical events
1845	Finishes first version of *L'Education sentimentale*; with the Flaubert family accompanies his sister on her honeymoon in Italy	Mérimée, *Carmen* Engels, *Condition of the Working-Class in England* Poe, *The Raven and Other Poems*	
1846	Death of father and sister; Flaubert now lives at Croisset with his mother and his sister's baby daughter, Caroline, whom he will bring up; meets Louise Colet in Paris, who becomes his mistress	Balzac, *La Cousine Bette* Proudhon, *La Philosophie de la Misère* Michelet, *Le Peuple*	
1847	Travels with Maxime Du Camp in Brittany; they record their impressions in *Par les champs et par les grèves*	Sand, *François le Champi* E. Brontë, *Wuthering Heights* C. Brontë, *Jane Eyre* Thackeray, *Vanity Fair*	Economic crisis, opposition campaign of reform banquets
1848	With Bouilhet and Du Camp witnesses February uprising in Paris; death of Alfred Le Poittevin; begins *La Tentation de saint Antoine*; breaks with Louise Colet	Chateaubriand, *Mémoires d'outre-tombe* Dumas fils, *La Dame aux camélias* Marx–Engels, *Manifesto of the Communist Party* Pre-Raphaelite Brotherhood founded	Year of revolutions in Europe February: overthrow of July Monarchy, institution of Second Republic; May–June: failure of 'National Workshops', Paris workers revolt crushed by troops; triumph of 'the party of order', Louis-Napoleon elected President

	Flaubert's life	Literature and the arts	Historical and cultural events
1848–52			Second Republic
1849	Reads *La Tentation* to Bouilhet and Du Camp who pronounce against it; leaves for tour of Middle East with Du Camp (Egypt, Palestine, Syria, Lebanon, Rhodes, Asia Minor, returning through Greece and Italy)	Sainte-Beuve, first 'Lundi' Sand, *La Petite Fadette* Dickens, *David Copperfield*	Elections: defeat of moderate republicans; workers' demonstrations, new heightening of repression
1850		Marx, *The Class Struggle in France: 1848–1850* Hawthorne, *The Scarlet Letter* Tennyson, *In Memoriam*	Law restricting suffrage Death of Louis-Philippe
1851	Returns to Croisset; starts new affair with Louise Colet; 19 September: begins writing *Madame Bovary*; witnesses December *coup d'état* in Paris	Goncourt brothers begin *Journal* Nerval, *Voyage en Orient* Beecher Stowe, *Uncle Tom's Cabin* Melville, *Moby Dick* Hugo in exile (1851–70)	Louis-Napoleon proposes revision of Constitution to allow his re-election, refused by parliament December: *coup d'état* extends presidential authority Great Exhibition in London
1852		Gautier, *Emaux et camées* Monnier, *Grandeur et décadence de Monsieur Joseph Prudhomme* Marx, *The Eighteenth Brumaire of Louis Bonaparte*	New Constitution; Louis-Napoleon becomes emperor as Napoleon III Creation of large financial institutions (*Crédit Foncier*)

Flaubert's life and works	Literary events	Historical events
1852–70		Second Empire
1853	Hugo, *Les Châtiments* Michelet, completion of *Histoire de la Révolution française*	Beginning of Haussmann's reconstruction of Paris
1854 Breaks definitively with Louise Colet	Barbey d'Aurevilly, *L'Ensorcelée* Champfleury, *Les Bourgeois de Molinchart*	Crimean War (1854–6). Pius IX proclaims dogma of the Immaculate Conception
1855	Nerval, *Aurélia* R. Browning, *Men and Women* Trollope, *The Warden* Whitman, *Leaves of Grass* Courbet, 'Du réalisme' exhibition of refused paintings	Exposition universelle in Paris
1856 Publication of *Madame Bovary* in the *Revue de Paris*; second version of *La Tentation de saint Antoine*, fragments published in *L'Artiste*	Duranty ed., *Le Réalisme* Hugo, *Les Contemplations*	Birth of the Prince Imperial, height of the Empire and the Imperial Court
1857 Trial of *Madame Bovary*, Flaubert and the *Revue de Paris* acquitted; publication and success of *Madame Bovary* in book form; begins *Salammbô*	Baudelaire, *Les Fleurs du Mal* (and trial, condemned) Champfleury, *Le Réalisme* E. B. Browning, *Aurora Leigh*	Anglo-French interventions in China

	Flaubert's life		Historical and cultural events
1858	Visits Tunisia to gather material for *Salammbô*	E. Feydeau, *Fanny* Michelet, *L'Amour*	Attempt by Orsini on Napoleon III's life; *loi de sûreté générale*
1859		Hugo, *La Légende des siècles* (first series) Michelet, *La Femme* Darwin, *The Origin of Species* Mill, *On Liberty* Tennyson, *Idylls of the King*	Beginning of construction of Suez Canal (1859–69) Franco-Austrian War (1859–60)
1860		Baudelaire, *Les Paradis artificiels* Dickens, *Great Expectations* Eliot, *The Mill on the Floss*	
1861			American Civil War (1861–5)
1862	Publication of *Salammbô*, great success; Flaubert now a literary personality, often in Paris	Fromentin, *Dominique* Hugo, *Les Misérables* Leconte de Lisle, *Poèmes barbares* First 'Magny' dinner Turgenev, *Fathers and Sons*	Bismarck appointed chief minister of Prussia
1863	Beginning of friendship with George Sand	Taine, *Histoire de la littérature anglaise*	

	Flaubert's life and works	Literary events	Historical events
1864	Begins second *Education sentimentale*; frequents the Princess Mathilde's Paris *salon*, received by the emperor at Compiègne	E. de Goncourt, *René Mauperin* Dickens, *Our Mutual Friend*	Foundation in London of International Working Men's Association (First International)
1866	Awarded *Légion d'honneur*	Verlaine, *Poèmes saturniens* Dostoevsky, *Crime and Punishment*	Foundation of *Société pour la Revendication des Droits de la Femme*, first French feminist organisation
1867		Zola, *Thérèse Raquin* Ibsen, *Peer Gynt* Marx, *Capital* (first volume)	Exposition universelle in Paris Troops sent to defend Rome against Garibaldi Second Reform Act (England)
1869	Publication of *L'Education sentimentale*; death of Bouilhet	Lautréamont, *Les Chants de Maldoror* Mallarmé, *Hérodiade* Mill, *The Subjection of Women* Tolstoy, completion of *War and Peace*	Elections, growth of liberal and republican oppositions Creation of *Ligue du Droit des Femmes*
1870	Begins third version of *La Tentation de saint Antoine*; Prussians billeted at Croisset		Franco-Prussian War; battle of Sedan, fall of the Empire; proclamation of Third Republic; siege of Paris

1870–1940

			Third Republic
1871	Flaubert renounces *Légion d'honneur* in response to armistice	Rimbaud writes *Le Bateau ivre* Darwin, *The Descent of Man* Eliot, *Middlemarch* Marx, *The Civil War in France*	Armistice and capitulation of Paris; Paris Commune
1872	Death of mother; completes *La Tentation*; begins to plan *Bouvard et Pécuchet*	Nietzsche, *The Birth of Tragedy*	Law against First International
1873	Growing friendship with Maupassant; writes *Le Candidat* (play)	Rimbaud writes *Une Saison en enfer* Verne, *Le Tour du monde en quatre-vingts jours* Pater, *Studies in the History of the Renaissance*	Death of Napoleon III Withdrawal of Prussian troops from France Mac-Mahon President of the Republic, elected by predominantly Royalist parliament
1874	*Le Candidat* fails after four performances in Paris; publication of *La Tentation*; begins writing *Bouvard et Pécuchet*	Barbey d'Aurevilly, *Les Diaboliques* Hardy, *Far from the Madding Crowd* Trollope, *The Way We Live Now* First Impressionist Exhibition	
1875	Financial difficulties as result of help given to his niece and her husband; begins *La Légende de saint Julien l'Hospitalier*	James, *Roderick Hudson*	Constitutional laws for the Republic

	Flaubert's life and works	Literary events	Historical events
1876	Completes *Saint Julien*; death of Louise Colet and George Sand; writes *Un Cœur simple*; begins *Hérodias*	Mallarmé, *L'Après-Midi d'un faune* Twain, *The Adventures of Tom Sawyer*	Elections, republican majority Queen Victoria proclaimed Empress of India Bell's telephone
1877	Completes *Hérodias*; the three stories are published together in a volume as *Trois Contes*; returns to *Bouvard et Pécuchet*	Zola, *L'Assommoir* Tolstoy, completion of *Anna Karenina*	Edison's phonograph
1879	Appointed *bibliothécaire hors cadre*, a sinecure position with a pension of 3,000 francs a year	Zola, *Nana* Dostoevsky, *The Brothers Karamazov* Ibsen, *A Doll's House*	Grévy elected President of the Republic, moderate republican government Reinstatement of the *Marseillaise* as national anthem
1880	8 May: death of Flaubert at Croisset	Zola, *Le Roman expérimental* *Les Soirées de Médan* (including Maupassant's *Boule-de-Suif*) Villiers de l'Isle-Adam, *L'Eve future* ('livre premier')	Amnesty for Communards 14 July becomes national holiday
1881	Publication of *Bouvard et Pécuchet* (unfinished); sale and demolition of the Croisset house		

Introduction

'The novelist's novelist', wrote Henry James of Flaubert, declaring *Madame Bovary* his masterpiece. Novelist and masterpiece have been decisively influential and remain an inescapable – at times obsessive – fact of modern literary experience. Doubtless the most remarkable testimony to this is the massive study of Flaubert as author of *Madame Bovary* undertaken by the philosopher Jean-Paul Sartre and still unfinished at his death, after nearly 3,000 pages. Conceptions of the book have varied strongly and importantly: Zola saw it as providing 'the code of the new art' he was developing as naturalism; Nabokov regarded it as essentially 'a prose poem'; Robbe-Grillet today considers it 'a *nouveau roman* before its time', unsettling our assumptions of realism and initiating a whole modern 'practice of writing'.

From the start, moreover, Flaubert's novel had an intense *social* reverberation. Brought to trial for offences against family and religion, it gained a notoriety that focused it at once as part of a questioning of marriage, sex, and the role of women. Its achievement was to transpose those given social elements into a new configuration that captured and articulated a fundamental experience of the post-romantic, commercial–industrial, democratic period. Indeed, the depiction of Emma Bovary was appropriated as a *general* representation and *bovarysme* entered French and other Western languages as the word for a typical attitude and its understanding. The disturbing aspect of the achievement, to which the trial was one response, involved quite directly Flaubert's artistic creed of impersonality, which was perceived as leaving his work

1

dangerously indifferent, with no clear moral, no message; only what Nietzsche would call 'the desire for nothing' and D. H. Lawrence condemn as a withdrawal from life 'as from a leprosy'. Nietzsche's attack bore too on *Madame Bovary* as exemplary of what he considered the damaging 'feminisation' of modern art and feeling, on the terms of its presentation of − its own implication in − *bovarysme*.

The story of the novel is briefly told: Emma Rouault becomes Madame Bovary, is disappointed in the marriage, has two affairs, catches herself inextricably in a mesh of debts, commits suicide. Its world is that of the provincial life so familiar to Flaubert, and the dissatisfaction with the marriage expresses an overall dissatisfaction with that world, a yearning for *something else* that the affairs cannot give, themselves in the end mere repetitions of the same banality. It is in the writing − in the *style*, to take Flaubert's word for the realisation of artistic vision, for the strength of the conversion of reality into art − that this simple material is produced as a richly complex work. Flaubert is close to Emma, *is* Madame Bovary, yet is also at the distance of his novel, is *Madame Bovary* as well as its heroine, is the writer–artist she cannot be. Through her, he records what he too knows as the disillusion that being in this world entails, a withdrawal from life indeed where 'life' in the first instance is the all-englobing reality of their bourgeois society; through the novel, he seeks to attain a value nevertheless, that of art (or Art, the capital letter stressing the value it is), proposed as sole possible fulfilment, sole possible truth to which one therefore owes exclusive commitment − Flaubert duly retreating to the room of his own in single-minded service to style. But then the ideal of art brings an intense problem of writing, since Flaubert the recluse is still bound to his age, entangled in its language and forms, held to a reality that threatens to overtake his novel, as Emma is overtaken, at every phrase. How is style to be secured, the novel made good as art, the distance gained from Emma and her − and his − world? It is these tensions that we read in *Madame Bovary*, that are the matter of its richness.

Hence the story of the novel is also the story of its writing in a quite unprecedented way. 'I am a pen-man', declares Flaubert soon after beginning *Madame Bovary* (31 January 1852, C), and indeed he is, living in and through and for words, the right words, suffering in solitude a whole martyrdom of creation. In his correspondence during the years of composition, he details in page after page, letter after letter, his torments as a writer, his conception of style, his literary opinions, his problems with the novel in hand. The letters were personal outpourings, the very antithesis of what art should be, in no way for publication: to insist on impersonality was to insist on the work as self-sufficient, separate from the artist's particular life and beliefs. Where a James would write prefaces to his own novels, essays on the art of fiction, innumerable critical reviews, Flaubert wrote nothing of the kind: readers in 1856 had only the novel, had none of Flaubert's ideas which were precisely elsewhere, in these − private − letters. Yet the latter have since been made available and we now read them too, know their extraordinary documentation of the years of *Madame Bovary*. Without reducing the novel to the letters, there is insight to be gained from grasping it with them in such a way as to understand the particular ideas and meanings and feelings that make up its determining context. How, from where, can Flaubert's identification with Madame Bovary be made? What is at stake in the calling of art? And in the writing of *this* novel, the masterpiece of the novelist's novelist?

Chapter 1

Madame Bovary: composition and context

Writing *Madame Bovary*

'What a damned profession! What an infernal obsession!'
(5 March 1853, C)

Flaubert began writing *Madame Bovary* on the evening of 19 September 1851; on the last day of May 1856 he sent the final manuscript to his friend Maxime Du Camp for publication in the *Revue de Paris*. His novel thus represents almost five years of a labour of composition that has become the very example of literary creation, of the vocation of the writer as artist. Two people shared in something of the trials of this labour: Louis Bouilhet, the Rouen schoolfriend, himself a poet, to whom the work in progress was read on Sundays; Louise Colet, the mistress, herself a poet and author, the recipient in Paris of the expression of Flaubert's passion of writing as recorded in more than 180 extant letters from 1851 onwards. When they broke up in 1854 and the letters came to an end, Flaubert was at the episode of the club-foot, the terms of the novel were set. *Madame Bovary*, indeed, was written to the rhythm of their relationship; or rather, the relationship was carried on to the rhythm of its writing, with meetings as and when this and then that section was completed; 'We won't see each other before. . .' became a constant refrain.

To write to Colet was to write to 'the eiderdown on which my heart comes to rest and the handy desk on which my mind can open' (27 February 1853, C). The letters are lengthy, mostly written late at night after the hours of struggle with the novel, as a respite from style: 'it's so easy to chatter on about the beautiful but to say in good style "close the door" or "he wanted to sleep" requires more genius than giving all the

4

literature courses in the world' (28 June 1853, C). If in the first
three months or so of 1853 Flaubert drafted thirty-nine pages
of *Madame Bovary*, in the same period he wrote some twenty-
three letters to Colet; that of 27 March, for example, running
to well over 4,000 words. Untiringly he set out his ideas on
the novel in hand and on art in general: 'one must esteem a
woman, to write her such things as these' (23 October 1851,
C). But then Colet was also a fellow-writer, already an established literary figure on the Paris scene. At the same time that
Emma Bovary in her convent would have been delicately
handling the satin bindings of keepsakes — elegant albums for
women — before blowing back the tissue paper over the prints
and losing herself in the world of romance, Colet was contributing to them. *Le Royal Keepsake* of 1842, dedicated 'Aux
Femmes', contains her 'Qui est-elle?', the pathetic story of 'a
pure woman' who, learning that for years she has been the
object of a famous painter's hopeless passion, comes to his
sick-bed, disguised as a nun, and gives herself to him in an act
of blameless redemption, keeping her identity for ever
unknown. At the same time that Flaubert was working on his
novel, Colet was publishing volumes of poetry with titles such
as *Ce qui est dans le cœur des femmes* (1852) and *Ce qu'on
rêve en aimant* (1854), and reproaching him as someone who
'will always have feeling yield to art'. He indeed was offering
correction after correction to her poems, trying to counter her
use of art as 'emotional outlet', hardening her style against 'the
female element' — 'only be a woman in bed' (4 September
1852, C). The commitment must be to art, not sentiment, to
art as a calling with style as its aim. Against Colet's fluency,
the letters record the pangs of art, give us the torment and
something of the terms of the writing of *Madame Bovary*,
documenting both the difficulties of this or that episode and
those of the overall conception of the novel.

The novel was written in seclusion at Croisset, Flaubert shut
in his room, nothing but work, drafting and redrafting in an
apparently interminable grind: 'in four days I've done five
pages' (16 January 1852, C); 'for my whole week three pages'
(26 June 1852, C); 'this whole week in which I've written about

one page' (3 July 1852, C). Even then the pages may not survive: 'four whole days for one really good page that I'm cutting . . . because it's out of place' (28 November 1852, C). Composition turned first and foremost on the agony of sentences, 'real tortures to write the simplest sentence' (2 November 1852, C). The sentence is the unit of style, the unit of work, the unit of life: 'the rage for sentences has dried up your heart' his mother informed him (27 June 1855, B). When the sentence will not come, he lies 'dazed, inwardly bogged in despair'; when it does, the satisfaction has a sexual intensity, Flaubert talking of 'ceaselessly masturbating [his] head so as to ejaculate sentences' (28 October 1853, C). The sentence is like the line in poetry, requiring the same concern with the placing of words, the avoidance of assonances and repetitions, the variation of pauses; but where poetry has its rules and defined forms, its established poetics, prose is a new and arduous terrain for art: 'How many repetitions of words I have just caught! . . . That is what is diabolical about prose, it's never finished!' (28 June 1853, C). Sentence and style, moreover, can be a trap: 'This book, which is only in style, has style itself as its continual danger. Intoxicated by the sentence, I lose sight of the idea' (23 January 1854, C). As paragraphs are tightened to perfection, so they at once need to be 'unscrewed', loosened to allow movement from one to the next, and so on and on, impossibly. 'So where is style? What does it consist in? I no longer know what it means. And yet, and yet I do! I feel it in my stomach' (29 January 1853, C). Only a saint would take on the atrocious, fanatical labour style requires: 'I love my work with a frenetic, perverted love, as the ascetic loves the hair shirt that scratches his belly' (24 April 1852, C).

Flaubert's priority is art over life, his commitment as artist *is* this fanaticism of style; at the same time, *Madame Bovary* is proposed as 'a reasonable book' (21 October 1851, MDC). Precisely. The subject is ordinary, provincial, bourgeois; everything is in the art, the style, the artist's work. Yet how reasonable can art be? How far can this subject sustain his ambition for style? The running complaint of the letters concerns the fetidness of the matter of the novel, the novelist 'dealing in shit' (21 September 1853, C). Flaubert is sick of it, physically sick; it sends him into a hysteria of *ennui*, with difficulties in breathing, wanting to vomit at table, a full complement of symptoms. From the novel he is engaged on to the age in which he lives and back again, everything is stifling; he, like Emma, cries for 'Air!' (15 July 1853, Victor Hugo). As far as his writing is concerned, this translates into a constant preoccupation with how to write the mediocre well. Form and content are inseparable, *and yet* form and content clash; there are no beautiful subjects, everything is in the art, *but* this novel will never be beautiful because of its subject, *but* the artist can transmute the ugliness of that, *but* then again. . . and so on and on in Flaubert's circle of endeavour and despair.

What is style? The internal strength, the *force* of a work. Only a few months after beginning 'the reasonable book', Flaubert is writing:

What seems beautiful to me, what I should like to write, is a book about nothing, a book dependent on nothing external, which would hold up on its own by the internal strength of its style, just as the earth, with no support, holds up in the air; a book which would have almost no subject, or at least in which the subject would be almost invisible, if such a thing is possible. The finest works are those that contain the least matter. . . I believe that the future of Art lies in this direction. I see it growing ever more ethereal.   (16 January 1852, C)

Art has priority over life, style is the term of this, the transformation of the real, but also an object in itself, hence the possibility – the ideal – of a book about nothing. Here is a fundamental aspect of the impersonality on which Flaubert lays such stress: the work must hold up on its own, dependent on nothing external and so free from any ties with its author's person.

Madame Bovary is conceived too with a more immediate impersonality, that of its very subject. This is not *my* book, insists Flaubert, contrasting it with his previous literary project, *La Tentation de saint Antoine*, a cosmic prose poem relating the temptations of the fourth-century desert father: 'In *Saint Antoine* I was at home, here I'm at the neighbour's' (13 June

1852, C). If Flaubert can refer to *Madame Bovary* as an 'exercise', it is inasmuch as it represents what he understands as a deliberate movement from the personal to the impersonal, from lyric flow to the hard muscle of making sentences, achieving style. The reasonable book is to mark a break with what went before: gone is the previous ease of *his* style ('dithyrambic and puffed-up', 2 June 1853, C), the loss of which Flaubert laments time and time again as he struggles with his new novel and its fetid, ordinary matter.

'Take a down-to-earth subject, one of those incidents of which bourgeois life is full.' Such was the advice given to Flaubert by Du Camp and Bouilhet in 1849 and which was one beginning of *Madame Bovary*. The advice followed the reading aloud to them of *La Tentation*: thirty-two hours over four days of this just-completed book in which Flaubert had only had to let himself go, free to indulge in lyricism to excess. *La Tentation* indeed was to stay with him for the rest of his life, always in his thoughts, always to be started over again; the day he announced the sending of the manuscript of *Madame Bovary* to Du Camp he also announced that he was reworking *La Tentation*, some extracts from which were then published in the journal *L'Artiste* in the weeks immediately following the last instalment of Emma's story in the *Revue de Paris*. In 1849, however, Bouilhet declares that *La Tentation* should be thrown on the fire and forgotten; Flaubert sets out on his trip to the East under the shock of this blow and returns to write *Madame Bovary*, down-to-earth, *terre à terre*.

1830–1850

'alias the last romantic fool' (3 February 1880, Léon Hennique)

Writing to Sainte-Beuve, the most eminent critic of the day, in gratitude for his important review of *Madame Bovary*, Flaubert defined himself as a 'vieux romantique enragé': 'I'm a rabid old romantic, or a fossilised one, whichever you prefer' (5 May 1857). Sainte-Beuve had spoken of the emergence of a new generation of writers, so many anatomists, physiologists, realists; which prompted Flaubert to make 'a purely personal point' in his letter: 'Don't judge me by this novel. I do not belong to the generation you speak of, at least that's not where my heart is. I'm insistent on belonging to yours, the good generation, that of 1830.' The 'good generation' here is that of the great moment of French romanticism which Flaubert, in fact younger than Sainte-Beuve by some seventeen years, experienced not in adulthood but in childhood and youth; the 1830s were formative years, but he was of the generation that came of age in the 1840s (Flaubert, like Baudelaire, was twenty-one in 1842) and wrote in the context of the 1850s, after the experience of 1848.

Had Flaubert written nothing after the first version of *L'Education sentimentale*, completed in 1845, he would stand for us as an interesting but minor romantic author. His numerous youthful writings include historical dramas, fantastic mystico-philosophical tales, and autobiographical narratives; with a taste for the heights of emotion, horror, spectacle, colour. His heroes and heroines are beings desperately in thrall to some exorbitant passion – an adulterous woman who kills husband and children in her delirium for her lover (*Passion et vertu*), a human ape who rapes and kills in his frustrated love (*Quidquid Volueris*). The compulsion of desire is expressed in long reveries of escape, 'limitless daydreams' of distant 'exotic' lands: 'Oh! to feel oneself swaying on the back of a camel!' (*OC* I, 271). Coupled with which is the disillusionment inherent in this 'frenzied race of the imagination', these 'ardent yearnings' (*OC* I, 249); a frustration that comes down inevitably to a wearied disgust with life: 'Very young, I had a complete premonition of life. It was like some nauseating smell of cooking' (7 April 1846, MDC).

Yearnings and frustration crystallise around the idea of a great love, an idea which the autobiographical narratives (*Mémoires d'un fou, Novembre*) intensely record, drawing on the fourteen-year-old Flaubert's encounter with Elisa Foucault on holiday in Trouville in 1836 (Elisa, twenty-five, was there with her husband-to-be and their child). What the encounter gave Flaubert was his image of *the* woman, the passion of an essence *woman* that Elisa represented but that no woman could be, that can have no reality − it is precisely fantasy − other than as loss, impossibility (Flaubert in his forties claimed still to be a virgin: none of the women he had slept with were *this* woman, the sole truth of his desire). Such an impossibility sums up that general experience of frustration and disgust − 'isn't happiness a metaphor invented one day of boredom?' (*OC* I, 252). At the same time as the idea of love and the woman, Flaubert is thus also writing out a negative metaphysics, an anathema on life, in a series of works (*Rêve d'enfer, La Danse des morts, Smarh*) whose vision is that of the world of human doings seen from on high with Satan as guide to this − his − kingdom: 'the world is hell' (this from the brief 1835 *Voyage en enfer, OC* I, 42). The only expression of any fulfilment is provided by the theme of the pantheistic experience of nature as 'total harmony', the revelation of a universal order − an immense sympathy of things and beings − whose laws are outside human understanding, 'that ecstasy alone can hear' (*OC* I, 257). Flaubert from early on feels himself able to enter into a stone or an animal, to become nature in passionate realisation of its harmony − 'the brother in God of everything that lives' (26 August 1846, C). Traces of this pantheism can be found in *Madame Bovary* in the moments of vibrant silence known by Emma in the forest when she yields to Rodolphe (II, 9) or in the garden with him, beneath the stars, on their nightly encounters (II, 10).

For a number of reasons romanticism came late in France, lagging behind its major developments in Germany and England. Innovation was difficult in a country where literature was so powerfully institutionalised, regulated through academies, official theatres, and so on. Moreover, the Revolutionary and Napoleonic periods were hostile to any attack on canonical French models in favour of foreign ones − Shakespeare versus Racine − and the 1789 Revolution anyway dispersed the literary audience into exile and emigration, breaking up the *salons* that could have provided the initiating context for the new literature. What the Revolution offered too was a full-scale public political action whose sheer historical significance overwhelmed the development of romantic feeling and art in any more intimate, more reflectively personal form. Struggles and desires were out on the streets, which demanded and produced an emphatic rhetoric of language and gesture, their own huge grandeur of meaning; the call was to the moment, making journalism or declamation or song the significant modes and leaving little time or place for other developments. Where art was concerned, the first years of the century were thus characterised mainly by a neo-classical consolidation of forms, styles and images, appropriate to the high matter of Republic and then of Empire.

The romanticism that subsequently emerged was profoundly marked by its position within the aftermath of this history and carried with it, almost from the start, something of its own disillusionment. 'Bliss was it in that dawn to be alive', wrote Wordsworth in 'The Prelude' in 1805 of the beginning of the French Revolution, recording how 'the meagre, stale, forbidding ways/Of custom, law, and statute took at once/The attraction of a country in romance!' For the French romantics that dawn was past; their reality was the trauma of the unfolding of the Revolution and the abandonment of its principles with the establishment of the Empire, followed by the triumph of the bourgeoisie when the July Revolution of 1830 led not to the enactment of republican ideals, but to the consecration of the authority of capital − to 'the bourgeois king' Louis-Philippe, the power of the financial aristocracy, and a social religion of self-enrichment through work and saving, *enrichissez-vous*. . .

Romanticism had had an initial conservative and catholic inflection, articulated by those − the exiles and émigrés − in opposition to the Revolution and its celebration of reason. Under the Restoration it gained a directly liberal and republican orientation, speaking for liberty and artistic and social renewal. 'Romanticism', wrote Hugo in the 'Préface' to *Hernani*, just months before the July Revolution, 'is, all in all, only liberalism in literature.' The ambition to play an important political role was strong in some of its major figures: Hugo himself, committed to the achievement of a liberal and humanitarian democracy, became a member of the French parliament in 1848; Lamartine, inspired by a liberal Christian social vision and deeply critical of the Louis-Philippe regime, was a member from 1833, serving as Minister of Foreign Affairs in the provisional government that in 1848 proclaimed the short-lived Second Republic. Such a romanticism of social ideals translating directly into political action could not survive the failures of 1848: Hugo went into exile after the *coup d'état* of December 1851; Lamartine, who stood against Louis-Napoleon in the presidential elections of 1848, had his parliamentary career ended with the coming of the Second Empire.

The politics of romanticism through the years of the July Monarchy was real, but romanticism was at the same time a powerful frustration with and turning away from the social–political sphere. Images of revolt were just that, only images, moving into the margins of mystery and melodrama to end in a purely literary violence of extremes; aspirations stretched elsewhere, turned to escapism; nature and self were cultivated in separation from the society and its politics, this separation being the very condition of any authenticity. The given reality was that of the bourgeois as established social order and all-pervasive ideology, against which romanticism now enacted a vague emotional agitation, an unsettled purposeless yearning, a bored lassitude, expressive of a *mal du siècle* that had quickly become so many 'attitudes', a fashion in feeling for the age, providing terms of experience and self-satisfaction for the sons and daughters and wives and artists of the very bourgeoisie itself.

Flaubert's early years can be measured out to the significant moments of the progression of romanticism in France. In 1820, the year before Flaubert was born, Lamartine published his *Méditations poétiques*, seeking to redefine poetry so as to render 'the very fibres of the human heart, touched and moved by the countless pulsations of soul and nature'; at the beginning of 1830, with Flaubert now eight, Hugo's play *Hernani*, inspired by Shakespeare and Schiller and breaking with classical rules, triumphed at the Comédie Française after a pitched battle between vociferous supporters and outraged opponents; in 1843, as Flaubert was beginning the first *Education sentimentale*, Hugo's *Les Burgraves*, a huge mythico-historical drama flopped in the same theatre, bringing the romantic curtain heavily down. The romanticism of the 1830s was Flaubert's adolescence: a dagger under his pillow, passionate admiration for Shakespeare and Hugo, absorption in Goethe's *Werther*, Chateaubriand's *René*, the poetry of Byron and Musset, extravagant dreams shared with the 'little group of hotheads' of his schooldays: 'our dreams were superb in their extravagance – the last effusions of romanticism reaching to us and, constrained by the provincial milieu, producing a strange seething in our brains' (*OC* II, 760). Like Emma Bovary's, his reading was full of lyricism, restlessness, the reverie of imagined worlds. Unlike her, though she in his writing of her comes to express this, he develops a distance from, a critique of these *fictions*, the fictions that romanticism comes to be seen to be. Nietzsche rightly insisted on Flaubert as the clearest French example of 'that typical transformation . . . in which romantic faith in love and the future is transformed into the desire for nothing, 1830 into 1850'. For Flaubert, writing in the 1850s, romanticism is part of a *modern* reality: it informs his thinking and feeling and being, his heart is with the 'good' generation of the 1830s; but it is also deeply problematic, ironised and attacked by him for its rhetoric, its illusions. 'Romanticism', wrote Baudelaire in his *Salon de 1846*, is art that is 'intimacy, spirituality, colour, yearning after the infinite', and these elements were crucial for Flaubert, he who 'was born lyrical' (25 October 1853, C). What is now felt, however, is a distrust of romanticism as their expression, its dismissal as merely romantic convention, a false imagination that is deflated by the reality that the writer – that Flaubert – *knows*. Flaubert's romantic reading is displaced on to Emma, set at that remove, and *Madame Bovary* is a manifesto of post-romanticism, scalpel not dream, written in contempt of 'consumptive lyricism' with its cohort of 'phrase-mongers, poseurs, swallowers of moonlight' (2 July 1853, C): 'Don't you feel that everything is now dissolving by *slackness*, moistness, tears, chit chat, milkiness? Literature today is drowned in women's periods. All of us need *to take iron* in order to get rid of the Gothic anaemia that Rousseau, Chateaubriand and Lamartine have transmitted to us' (15 January 1854, C). The need, in other words, is for a new, *impersonal* art.

Accompanying this is an intense hatred of all politics, bearing witness to the process of degeneration that characterises the contemporary history from 1830 to 1850 and beyond. What that history represents is the destruction of any possibility of belief in social renewal: ' '89 demolished royalty and the nobility, '48 the bourgeoisie and '51 *the people*. Now there is *nothing*, only a rascally and imbecile rabble. We are all sunk at the same level in a common mediocrity. Social equality has entered the sphere of the Mind. There are books for everyone, art for everyone, science for everyone, just as we build railways and heated public restrooms. Humanity has the frenzy for moral abasement. And I'm angry at it, because I'm part of it' (22 September 1853, C). Romanticism returns here as the decisive contradiction of Flaubert's writing, Flaubert operating what the critic Georg Lukács calls a 'dual critique': ironic detachment from his own ineradicable romanticism is coupled with rejection of a bourgeois world condemned by the standards of this same romanticism. Hearing of the charges against *Madame Bovary*, the novelist Jules de Goncourt explained to Flaubert that the intention was to ensure the death of romanticism, now become a 'crime against the State'. This can seem at first sight paradoxical: surely what is at stake is a reaction to the book's *realism*? But the point is that this realism is exactly the product of romanticism, the gesture of its historical collapse: there is only the one reality, that of the contemporary bourgeois world, and writing is in revolt against this reality, exposing it as it really is − realism as both recognition and refusal. The State, in Goncourt's analysis, wants the death of romanticism and so brings Flaubert's novel to trial for the critique − the realism − which that romanticism provokes.

The twist, the 'dual critique' again, is that realism is also an indictment of romanticism, the latter itself as degraded as the world it confronts and on whose terms it exists, with which it is thick. Romanticism and realism have their interrelations and are mutually critical and are both equally compromised. Flaubert's only value can be Art, art for art's sake, independent of the world; with impersonality as separation from any positioning of the self, and style as the specific task and mode of existence of the writer, away from all the mass-cultural commerce of 'literature'. When Flaubert imagines a book about nothing, longs to have only to write sentences, cites the impression left by a bare wall as an image for the effect he would like to achieve in a work, it is this idea of the object Art and of the art object that is being proposed, the work *as art* freed from implication in the facts and factions, values and validations of the century.

But none of this is calmly, easily achieved; retreat is the struggle of reaction. Baudelaire adopts dandyism as a mode of distance and defiance; Verlaine turns to absinthe and the pistol; Rimbaud loses himself in Abyssinia and the darkness of colonialism (it is with these figures that Flaubert must be compared, every bit as much as with Balzac, Zola and the figures of 'European realism'). Flaubert retires, quietly installed at Croisset, in hatred of the century that is his nevertheless, tired of it all, weary, bored. This is *his* politics, his politics of writing: demoralise, deal in shit, and transfigure, make art. The artist must be radically separate from the bourgeois, but the latter is the all-encompassing reality of contemporary social being, including that of the artist himself living in this society; so the artist can only be priest, ascetic, saint, vowed to solitude and dedicated to impersonality, renouncing social being, any expression of self.

Aged nine, Flaubert declares New Year's Day foolish and proposes to record the 'stupid things' that a visitor always says, 'I'll write them' (1 January 1831, EC); aged eleven, he notes 'Ah!!! How stupid the world is!' (11 September 1833, EC); aged fifteen, he comments 'I have lived, that is, I have been bored' (24 June 1837, EC); aged sixteen, he has come to 'look on the world as a spectacle and laugh at it' (13 September 1838, EC). Born bored, old on leaving the cradle, unable to take an active part in the world other than as 'a demoraliser', this is Flaubert's constant presentation of himself. As he explained to Du Camp when beginning *Madame Bovary*: 'My youth . . . steeped me in an opiate of boredom, sufficient for the remainder of my days. I hate life . . . I have dragged this feeling everywhere, through everything, wherever I have been: at school, in Rouen, in Paris, on the Nile' (21 October 1851). If romanticism came late in France, Flaubert came late in romanticism; aspiration and boredom go together from the start: illusions but without the illusion of the illusions, gestures at romanticism but with romanticism instantly anachronistic, no more than gestures, rhetoric, adolescence. Romantic lassitude now is a radical boredom with the stale commerce of existence. 'We were, a few years ago in the provinces, a constellation of young rascals . . . between madness and suicide. . . It had its beauty', Flaubert recalls at the time of *Madame Bovary*, in another evocation of his youth (3 November 1851, C); his novel now also looks back to school-days, starts with the same 'We were' – 'Nous étions' – and follows it with nothing but Bovary and *bovarysme*. The reality is bourgeois, resistance is in art alone.

Thinking of his youth, Flaubert always saw his life as cut in two, with illness as the decisive break. In January 1844, driving a carriage with his brother on a Normandy road, Flaubert fell as though struck by apoplexy. Other attacks followed, and it was agreed that Flaubert would have to give up his legal studies and the career and life to which family and class destined him. Those contemporaries who later mentioned the topic talked of epilepsy and some of Flaubert's descriptions of his attacks exactly match such a diagnosis, with which indeed modern medical assessments of the evidence generally concur. He, however, always talked of 'nerves', 'nervous crises', 'nervous attacks', perhaps in order to avoid the recognition and acknowledgement of epilepsy; but equally perhaps as an exact response to a hysteric neurosis that would have been even more difficult for the family of the respected Dr Flaubert to identify and diagnose in one of its sons. Who knows? 'No one has studied all that and doctors are a species of imbeciles' (7 July

1853, C). Whether epilepsy or epileptiform hysteria, however, it is certain that the illness served Flaubert's purpose, fitted only too well with the boredom and the disgust he felt at the world: 'My illness will have had one benefit, in that I am allowed to spend my time as I want' (January 1845, Emmanuel Vasse de Saint-Ouen). Now he could devote himself wholly to writing, bidding 'an irrevocable farewell to practical life' (13 May 1845, ALP).

The break comes as a division of chronological time − before and after − but can also be put in terms of personal existence − inner and outer: *'Break with the outside world*, live like a bear − a polar bear − let everything else go to hell − everything, yourself included, except your intelligence' (16 September 1845, ALP). One lives as a bourgeois but one thinks and works in a separate sphere, within oneself: 'practical dogma in the life of an artist . . . one must make two parts of one's existence' (21 August 1853, C). The illness confirms these two parts and the need for retreat, the artist's necessary isolation. At the same time this idea of two parts has a literary transposition, becomes Flaubert's very understanding of himself and his writing, divided between lyrical aspiration and realistic perception:

> There are in me, literarily speaking, two distinct persons: one who is infatuated with impassioned outbursts, lyricism, eagle flights, sonorities of phrase and lofty ideas; and another who digs and burrows into the truth as deeply as he can, who likes to treat a humble truth as respectfully as a big one, who would like to make you feel almost *physically* the things he reproduces.   (16 January 1852, C)

Of these two fundamental tendencies, Flaubert always insisted that the lyrical was deepest (friends such as Du Camp agreed). But abandonment to 'inspiration' is ruinous for art, which is not some 'chamberpot' for 'the foam of the heart', some 'outflow for passion' (22 April 1854, C). But then again passion is everywhere in Flaubert, for example in the same letter from which those last phrases were taken: 'Above all there must be *blood* in one's sentences, not lymph, and when I say blood, I mean *heart*. It needs to beat, throb, move.' The desire for nothing of which Nietzsche spoke is much more an immensity of desire for which there are no forms of realisation and which can be expressed only in terms of immensity, as an all-embracing force in and for itself: 'My desire is too universal, too permanent and too intense for me to have desires' (13 May 1845, ALP). Retreat, inner solitude, the asceticism of the artist are then, in fact, the mode of this desire, the condition of its unfettered enjoyment: to have nothing leaves desire free as value, sustains its universality.

Limited, desire is degraded into the particular forms of the social world, its commonplaces, those of romanticism included. Everything has been overtaken by the nineteenth century, this bourgeois civilisation and its version of things: 'stones even become stupid' (29 January 1854, C). There is nothing left but Art, the striving nonetheless for the truth of Form and Beauty, outside of the particular, the personal, the social, towards the transfiguration of the real. Art thus becomes the *possible* life for the modern writer–artist; but at a loss, which is what is tragic in Flaubert, as far from any simple version of 'art for art's sake' as from any simple nihilism of a desire for nothing. The greatest writers – Shakespeare, Cervantes, even Hugo, the last of the great – are said not to have needed art, since theirs was the supreme strength of life; it is the lesser writers – those of Flaubert's time – who are condemned to form and style, polishing sentences, sweating hours over a single word or comma: whatever strength they have will come from that labour alone. 'Life! Life! getting hard-ons, that is everything!' (15 July 1853, C); but that 'everything' of life, the lyricism that is its expression, is now condemned to the critique of the reality it faces, to a realism of 'the medical vision of life, that view of the true' (24 April 1852, C). Which brings us back to the new generation of anatomists, physiologists, realists recognised by Sainte-Beuve in *Madame Bovary*: a literature of the scalpel. The personal identification with the old – 'good' – generation which Flaubert was so concerned to stress was made from his actual situation in the contemporary one, the 1830s as nostalgia on the part of the writer of the 1850s, who simultaneously breaks off from just those earlier years and their convictions and conceptions. The wonderful time of Flaubert's youth, when he could dash off a play in a matter of days must give way to the time of the 'reasonable book', to *Madame Bovary* as medical vision and work of style. Being a modern writer is in the conjunction and contradictions of these terms of desire and impersonality and art: 'It is time to succeed or to throw myself out of the window' (16 January 1852, C).

The third attempt

'Now I am at my third attempt' (16 January 1852, C)

By the time Flaubert is twenty-one, everything is in place, everything potentially written; *Novembre* in 1842 marking for him the close of his youth. Between this close and the beginning of what he calls his 'third attempt' at aesthetic success with *Madame Bovary* in 1851, the first novel he will publish, there have been the two other attempts: *L'Education sentimentale* (1843–5, not to be confused with the quite different novel of the same title that will appear in 1869) and *La Tentation de saint Antoine* (1848–9).

L'Education sentimentale tells its story of such an education through the lives of two young men, Henry and Jules. The first comes to study law in Paris, succumbs to the poetry of adultery and elopes with his lover in a passion which inevitably turns to the usual banality: absorbed into the social world, Henry disappears into 'the common hue'. The second stays in his provincial town, falls dupe to a love that has no truth other than his desire and is brought to a 'considered despair': left solitary, maintaining only 'a conviction in the ideal', Jules ends in self-dedication to art. The autobiographical element is clearly strong. What is new is the artistic elaboration that Flaubert begins to give his experience, breaking somewhat with the more strictly confessional mode of *Mémoires d'un fou* and *Novembre*. There is much here already of *Madame Bovary*: in the details of the adultery; in this or that character (Henry, who at the end takes on something of the mediocre cynicism of Rodolphe); in the demonstration of the emptiness of the society through its language, its clichés (Henry's father looks forward to Homais, displaying himself with the latter's sententious complacency); in the very idea of a sentimental education, which fits Emma's story as well, but with the great difference that she, unlike Jules, has no recourse in art. Unlike Gustave too, who sees his own life in similar terms: 'I have voluntarily weaned myself from so many things that I feel rich in the midst of the most absolute destitution. . . My sentimental education isn't over yet but I am near the end perhaps' (17 June 1845, ALP). He wrote that just after finishing *L'Education sentimentale*, which itself finishes with Jules in much the same situation; the novel and the life go together in this consciousness of a necessary movement through disillusionment to renunciation and impersonality.

The phrase itself, 'sentimental education', is found only once in *L'Education sentimentale*, in a condensed, definitive passage that sets down the life of a black man in rags encountered on the boat taking Henry and his mistress to New York:

His father had sold him for a packet of nails; he had come to France as a servant, he had stolen a scarf for a chambermaid he loved, he was sent to the hulks for five years; he had come back from Toulon to Le Havre on foot to see his mistress again, he had not found her, now he was going back to the black men's country. He had done his sentimental education.   (*OC* I, 333)

All Flaubert is there: the derisiveness of an existence without value, merely contingent, worth a packet of nails; the futility of a passion that was only ever an illusion, the woman cannot be found and would anyway never have been what she was imagined to be; the oppressive constraint of the social world, one of servitude and imprisonment; the fatal narrative of this, clause following clause in a story that allows of no appeal – such was this man's sentimental education and ours will be no different. All Flaubert except for art. But then what if art itself, the recourse in that, were only another illusion, equally futile, equally derisory? Statoë, the black man, sits carving 'the portrait of the emperor on coconut shells'; like Binet in *Madame Bovary* with his lathe and his convoluted napkin rings, like Flaubert turning his endlessly polished sentences. . .

L'Education sentimentale straddles the decisive period that

Flaubert's illness punctuates and inflects, setting him apart, confirming the desired retreat from law to Art, Henry to Jules. From 1843 to 1845 his life is decided, those two years of illness and writing have brought him near to an end, his sentimental education is almost over, what is to come will be *after*, in full knowledge of Henry and Jules and Statoë. After, but then the past, all the desire, is still there. In 1845–6, Flaubert is working on 'an oriental story', a philosophical fable on the quest for happiness, ending inevitably in failure, that plunges him into 'colour, poetry, what is sonorous, warm, beautiful' (15 September 1846, Vasse de Saint-Ouen). In May 1848, his beloved sister and his father now dead, in the midst of the political and social upheavals of the time, Flaubert begins what will be the second attempt before *Madame Bovary, La Tentation de saint Antoine.*

This is the book that he will always stress as having been written with his 'entire self', the great book of unfettered impulse: 'a subject which left me completely free as to lyricism, movements, excesses' (16 January 1852, C). Disconcerting, ambiguous, *La Tentation* dramatises the temptations of the hermit saint in his desert cave. A whole array of gods, sects, beliefs, heresies are paraded before him, leaving no certitude save that of negation, which itself in this enigmatic text is no conclusion. At the same time, in the figure of the ascetic, Flaubert expresses desire raised to its highest power: the pious morality of the saint's resistance to the trials of his faith becomes in Flaubert's writing the luxurious enormity of the force of desire that ascesis provokes − the turning away from life responds to the fact of desire as boundless, as a movement of mind, spirit, imagination, outside of all constraints of body and world. Antoine's hallucinations are more real than any reality, have the truth of their intensity and sheer immensity. When Flaubert finally publishes *La Tentation* in a third version in 1874, he will make its conclusion the wish 'to be matter' (*OC* I, 571): fusion with the totality of being as the only true end for desire.

'A soul is to be measured by the extent of its desire' (21 May 1853, C); something to be remembered in the world of Emma

Bovary, which was already Flaubert's as he wrote those words. Madame Bovary is him, but so was Saint Antoine before her: 'I was myself Saint Antoine in *Saint Antoine*' (31 January 1852, C). Flaubert's too is this enormous, limitless desire, losing himself in fantastic dreams of being emperor of Indochina, having slaves, 6,000 wives. No object can meet this desire whose very essence is the strength of its aspiration beyond limits. All translation into reality, all possession, is deflation, desire reduced to the flat monotony of 'pleasures'. Not to sleep with a woman in the prostitutes' quarter of a town on the Nile is an example of 'stoical *artistism*', a way of keeping the desire intact in the imagination, of preserving the poetry of the scene. Indeed, even the longed-for, dreamed-of Orient is, when visited, for all the bedazzlement that Flaubert experiences, not really up to the desire, and Du Camp was no doubt right enough when he insisted on Flaubert's disappointment (the real trip cannot in the end match the trip Flaubert has already made a thousand times in fantasy, including in the writing of *La Tentation*). Thus we come back to the Flaubertian retreat, the separation from the world: it suffices to have nothing in order to have everything, the full dimension of desire in all its integrity; 'stoical artistism' rejoins Saint Antoine's asceticism, which in turn can be seen as an artistic mode. Sartre puts it well: 'Gustave will define himself through *desire*, that is to say, sumptuously and universally by everything he does not have . . . the great unappeasable desire is a destructuration of the ordinary man.' Art is now the only possible religion, and the impersonality it demands is no more nor less than the totalisation of desire, the modern artist–ascetic nowhere but *everywhere* present.

'What attracts me above all else is religion. I mean all religions, no one more than any other. Each dogma in particular is repulsive to me, but I consider the feeling that invented them as the most natural and poetic of humanity' (30 March 1857, LdC). It is the feeling that counts: 'the belief finally in something superior to life' (31 March 1853, C). Or in other words, the foundation of religion, its fundamental impetus, is human desire confronting the misery of being in this world:

'It is this disgust at our worthless existence that has led to the invention of religions, the ideal worlds of art' (19 September 1852, C). In the nineteenth century, the century of history (and of the history of religion into which Flaubert plunges for *La Tentation*), there can be no question of belief − 'I believe in nothing, not even in myself, which is rare' (6 or 7 August 1846, C) − other than in something like a perpetual evolution of humanity, a coming and going of forms far removed from any notion of 'progress', any human meaning. 'The infinite, moreover, overwhelms all our conceptions' (6 June 1857, LdC); truth for humankind lies in the recognition of its nescience: 'Be *more Christian*. And resign yourself to ignorance' (*ibid*). This necessary ignorance is another version of the impersonality at which art must aim. Art must show, set out, exhibit, which for Flaubert means be scientific: 'Let us try to see things as they are and not seek to be more intelligent than God . . . let us accustom ourselves to considering the world as a work of art whose procedures are to be reproduced in our works' (27 March 1853, C). A novel, for example, is to be written 'without love or hate for any of the characters' (7 October 1852, C), without any certainties: the artist 'should have no religion, no country, not even any social conviction', only 'absolute doubt' (26 April 1853, C). Or to put it another way again, the artist is to be occupied simply in the *matter* of existence, not in its explanation: 'We torture our minds trying to understand the abyss that separates it from us' (24 August 1853, B).

This is the − inhuman − sense of nature in Flaubert; it represents the abyss between human practice and the world: 'How little nature cares for us! And how impassive the look of the trees, the grass, the waves!' (14 August 1853, C). To look at a garden devastated by a storm is to see all of man's little arrangements for what they always are: purely factitious, meaningless. Inveterately, we pull things to us, make up the world in so many fictions, but the reality is beyond us, Nature or God takes revenge, recalls us by a storm or a plague or some other unexpected upheaval to 'the Law of "Being" ': 'something that men vowed to nothingness little understand' (12 July 1853, C). It is the sense too of rottenness, gangrene, corruption, putrefaction, of everything to do with our bodies of filth and decay: 'I have never seen a child without thinking that it would grow old, nor a cradle without thinking of the grave. The sight of a naked woman makes me imagine her skeleton' (6 or 7 August 1846, C). Stupidity is not in lyricism, aspiration, desire, it is in human platitude, the common terms of human self-satisfaction, all our *conclusions*: 'Yes, stupidity consists in wanting to reach conclusions. We are a thread and we want to know the whole design' (4 September 1850, B). The artist, on the contrary, is defined by resistance to any such fictions of finality: 'One must accept everything, resigned to not concluding' (18 December 1859, LdC).

Bouilhet saw in *La Tentation* an overflowing of the faculties of both irony and lyricism. Flaubert claimed, 'if anything', to be 'materialist–spiritual' (*SNPI*, 48), the two attitudes together: 'The materialists and the spiritualists equally prevent understanding of matter and mind, because they split the one from the other. The latter make man an angel, the former a pig' (7 July 1853, C). But under Flaubert's eye, there is very much of the pig; the spectator looking on, with the detachment of the artist, sees farce: 'When will the facts be written from the point of view *of a superior farce*, that is to say, as the good God sees them from on high?' (7 October 1852, C). Farce, joke, irony: 'the dismal grotesque holds immense charm for me, it corresponds to the intimate needs of my nature, buffoonishly bitter' (21–22 August 1846, C). Flaubert, twenty-three, is 'a curiously damaged fellow, with arse, legs and head in pulp: my skin will soon be no more than a huge red, suppurating sore – What a farce!' (July 1845, ALP). A wife betrays her husband with ever more lovers, 'while he grows more and more horns, she gets more and more horny – Farce, pun!' (2 March 1854, C). A servant in the house at Croisset tries 'to sodomise the gardener under a beech tree' (July 1857, JD) – more farce, with everything epitomised in that 'under a beech tree': the implacable ordinariness of it all, just under Flaubert's window, and the implacable indifference of things, against the ludicrousness of the human. Performer – like the blind man – of grotesque comic turns (favourites are 'the epileptic beggar', 'the howling dervish', 'the salon idiot'), Flaubert is always ready with a whole repertoire of ridicule — 'that ridicule intrinsic to human life itself and which comes out in the simplest action or the most ordinary gesture' (21–22 August 1846, C).

Intrinsic to human life itself, the ridicule is intrinsic especially to this nineteenth century in which, while belief is no longer possible, a whole host of beliefs have nevertheless been hardened into received truths, so many fictions of progress, democracy, civilisation. This ridicule has a name, *bêtise*, and a representative, *le bourgeois*, 'which is now to say, humanity in its entirety, the people included' (22 November 1852, C). 'The bourgeois' for Flaubert is not a simple political category, but the overall social–cultural reality, the triumphant universalisation of conclusions, stupidity at its height, spread everywhere by the mass-production of reading matter (Flaubert had a particular hatred of newspapers). Politically, therefore, there are no differences, everything is equally bourgeois, right down to socialism which is the very nadir of bourgeois stupidity, the exemplar of the general moral besottedness. 'Isn't the dream of socialism to have humanity sitting in some kennel all painted yellow, like a railway station, and that there it be, monstrously obese, waddling on its balls, drunk and blissful, with eyes closed, digesting its lunch, waiting for its dinner, and defecating under itself?' (2 March 1854, C). The enormity of the bourgeois, the aplomb of the omnipresent *bêtise*, is fascinating; Zola records how Flaubert showed him a collection of 'all the documents of human imbecility he could find'.

Enormity and fascination had their early and decisive figure, that of the *Garçon*, 'the Lad'. The *Garçon* was a character created by Flaubert and his Rouen schoolfriends, remaining a reference for him throughout his life. Grotesque, Rabelaisian, Ubuesque, 'a sort of modern Gargantua. . . in the skin of a commercial traveller' (in the words of Flaubert's niece, Caroline), the *Garçon* was an enactment of derision through grossness, both a compendium of everything bourgeois and a violence against it in his farcical behaviour, his boorish disrespect for manners and values. Writing to one of those schoolfriends, now a government official in Corsica, Flaubert describes how he would like to turn up one morning and 'smash and break everything, belch behind the door, upset the ink-stands and shit in front of the bust of His Majesty, in short make the *Garçon*'s entry' (13 July 1847, EC). The *Garçon* directs ridicule against others, but is also himself ridiculously grotesque: to act him was to scorn the bourgeois and to include oneself in the scorn. Flaubert and his friends fill the *Garçon*'s mouth with stereotypes and, as the *Garçon*, repeat those stereotypes, identify with the bourgeois they mock. Bourgeois themselves through and through (who could not be in Flaubert's vision of things?), they mimic everything bourgeois so as to explode it from inside by this inflationary repetition (what other strategy could there be?), but with the inflation simultaneously a homage to the power of the bourgeois (isn't the reality always more stupefyingly egregious?). Flaubert is as subject to cliché as the *Garçon* or any of his other characters (platitudes fall readily under his pen too: 'It is incredible how one meets acquaintances when travelling. At Smyrna we dined (and dined well) with doctors who knew our fathers by name', 24 November 1850, mother); Homais, a version of the *Garçon*, is not just distant, but also close to the novelist.

Stupidity is indeed everywhere, oozingly infectious − one should wear 'a huge internal condom' (18 January 1854, C). Everywhere including within oneself, condom notwithstanding. It is not simply that Flaubert lives 'the most bourgeois life on earth' (30 August 1846, C), it is that, like everyone else, he is caught in the century, its language, its stupidity. How can one escape? 'Tell me what is more stupid than what I've just written, if not the person writing it?' (21 December 1842). This joke to his sister Caroline is more than a joke; it is the twist of Flaubert's writing for the rest of his life. The only sense is 'absolute doubt', but then writing looks to become impos-sible: at any moment you may be caught by your very irony, pulled into certainty. And anyway 'absolute doubt' is itself a certainty, which gives another turn: 'I doubt everything, and even my doubt' (8–9 August 1846, C). Hence again the need for impersonality: no 'I', no position, no certainty, even of no certainty. A year before beginning *Madame Bovary*,

Flaubert is envisaging a book written in such a way 'that the reader won't know whether or not he is being made a fool of, yes or no' (4 September 1850, B). This is the *Garçon* refined into writing, another strategy of imitation involving an assembly of stereotypes, a dictionary of received ideas: 'There would not be a single word of mine in the whole book, done in such a way that once one had read it one would not dare to speak again, for fear of uttering naturally one of the sentences in it' (16 December 1852, C). What is needed in other words is an irony, a mode of writing, that will be totally elusive, undecidable, leaving no firm hold for the reader − but then would that be irony or repetition, indistinguishable from what was being copied?

Not a word of Flaubert's own. . . This idea of copying is a constant preoccupation, from the child's intention to note down the visitor's stupidities to *Bouvard et Pécuchet* on which Flaubert is still working at the time of his death, the book that had been with him for so much of his life, along with *La Tentation*, the two *together*: the book of emotion to excess, and the book of vengeance against the century. Flaubert's writing, indeed, can be easily classified by reference to lyricism and irony and their alternation: on the one hand, the romantic books, the extremes of desire, the imagination set loose (*La Tentation, Salammbô*); on the other, the realist books, constrained to the monochrome flatness of the social world observed and recorded (*Madame Bovary*, the second *Education sentimentale, Bouvard et Pécuchet*). Such a classification is true enough, but also misleading, so much do the same themes, the same pressures, run through all the books; and misleading especially for *Madame Bovary*, even if it was begun as 'a reasonable book' in reaction to the outlandish *Tentation*, good only for the fire. We need to bear in mind Flaubert's urging of Louise Colet 'to write a great novel. . . mixed with irony and feeling, that is to say true' (13 October 1846). Baudelaire after all, the finest reader of *Madame Bovary*, recognised at once beneath the novel's meticulous texture 'the high faculties of *lyricism* and *irony*' both.

Realism

'It was in hatred of realism that I undertook this novel' (30 October 1856, RdG)

The years of the writing of *Madame Bovary* are those of the emergence of 'realism' as an important literary and artistic term. In 1855 the painter Gustave Courbet had the words 'Du Réalisme' placed over the door of an exhibition of his paintings rejected by the official Salon and in 1857 the novelist Champfleury published a collection of essays under the title *Le Réalisme*, a title also used by fellow-novelist Edmond Duranty for a journal he ran from 1856–7. Balzac, the bulk of whose novels were written in the 1830s and 1840s (with publication of the programmatic 'Avant-Propos' to the *Comédie Humaine* in 1842), was being influentially described and discussed as a realist at this time, established as the key literary reference for realism; advising Flaubert to abandon *La Tentation* in favour of a down-to-earth subject, Bouilhet and Du Camp naturally cite Balzac's work as a model, 'something like *La Cousine Bette*, like *Le Cousin Pons*'. Yet as Champfleury himself pointed out even as he adopted it, 'realism' was an 'equivocal term', and one used more often by critics as a hostile reaction to new tendencies than by writers as a positive definition of their work. Baudelaire in his review of *Madame Bovary* in 1857 stigmatised it as 'a disgusting insult flung in the face of every analytical writer, a vague and elastic word which for common minds signifies not a new method of creation but a minute description of accessories'.

The equivocal term nevertheless had some prime meanings, of which the minute description of accessories was indeed one. Realism referred to the detailed treatment of the given world of people and things, this then being the limit of its vision: the ordinary, the everyday, no great – heroic, epic – figures or events; just the *human* comedy. As the subject-matter of literature was thus extended into hitherto excluded areas, dealing seriously now with 'lower' spheres of social life, so realism became synonymous too, another of its meanings, with the ugly, the scabrous, the sordid, a shocking refusal of the good and the ideal, a brutal subordination of morality to reality. Put positively, claimed as a new method of creation, realism involved a fundamental materialism: an account of the world as socio-historical reality within which, and only within which, are lives made, values defined, meanings found (there is no divine inspiration, no transcendence, God has left). The novel, as modern genre with an ever-increasing social distribution (the expanding market for its fictions), became the supreme literary form of this account and novelists conceived their work in terms of realism as the scientific study of society (using fictions to probe its nature and bring out its laws): Balzac called himself 'a doctor of social science' and referred to natural history as the model for his writing, for his parallel attempt to develop a fully social history; Zola, whose naturalism was offered as a more scientific version of realism, referred to experimental medicine and projected an 'experimental novel' in its image. Observation and analysis, the production of social understanding, the revelation of the workings and movements of society, these were the defining techniques and objectives. Realism could then also be given a politically progressive ambition: social understanding leading to social critique leading in turn to some democratic vision of necessary change.

Flaubert's idea of writing and of the writer—artist would have nothing to do with movements or schools: 'After the Realists, we have the Naturalists and the Impressionists. What progress! Bunch of clowns', as he wrote to the Russian novelist Turgenev towards the end of his life (8 December 1877). The refusal of any constituted school was shared too, however, by those closest to the explicit conception of realism as aim: 'I shun schools like the cholera' declared Champfleury, in words that might have been Flaubert's. Realism was proposed as anti-literary, by definition outside of any school; in Duranty's words, 'realism signifies the frank and complete expression of individualities; conventions, imitations, any kind of *school* are exactly what it attacks'. But this does not alter the fact that there emerged in literature and art in the 1850s a declared commitment to 'an *exact*, *complete*, and *sincere* reproduction of the social milieu, and the epoch in which one lives', Duranty's words again, his definition of realism nevertheless. It was in relation to the emergence of this commitment that *Madame Bovary* was received and, more often than not, attacked; this while Flaubert was asserting his hatred of realism and his disgust at ordinary life: 'They think I'm smitten with the real whereas I loathe it. For it was in hatred of realism that I undertook this novel. But no less do I detest the false idealisation with which we are lulled these days' (30 October 1856, RdG).

The hatred of realism is a hatred of the reality it represents. Flaubert's constant words during the writing of *Madame Bovary* are 'stupid', 'fetid' – 'the foulness makes me sick' – which apply both to the subject of the book he is writing and to the world around him, these being one and the same; one bourgeois reality from world to book and back again. How does one write in this world? Flaubert is involved in the novel of the 1850s despite himself, with realism as the necessary counter to the false idealism of romanticism and its empty rhetoric (Champfleury described the realists as being 'tired of versified lies, of the persistence of the tail-end romantics'). The paradoxical force of Flaubert's writing is then that realism, development and critique of romanticism, is itself equally subject to critique; the movement of disillusionment from romanticism to realism is also for him just as much a refusal of any of the illusions *of the latter*, of any of realism's social, progressive purpose: realism is as execrable as the reality it knows and depicts, is caught in the surrounding stupidity, the general fetidness. Flaubert is anti-realist at the heart of realism, with romanticism as the impetus and the edge of his critique, as the term for all the strength of desire negated by this bourgeois reality and by what is, for Flaubert, *its* realism. It is the distance from the given reality, exactly the execration of the ordinary life enacted in Emma's story, that counts and that produces the lack of value for which the novel is brought to trial: romanticism has become demoralisation, remaining nevertheless as an aspiration in reaction against this world whose reality it seeks to expose, to set out as it really is, with no concessions to any of its fictions of itself, thereby perpetrating that 'crime against the State'.

For this duality of realism/romanticism, the very situation of his writing, Flaubert then has his resolution, a resolution by displacement to another value: Art. Reality is to be set out as it is, but also transformed, is to serve as a 'spring-board' for style, for the *work* of art. Those who most powerfully claimed *Madame Bovary* as a realist–naturalist model found themselves at the same time obliged to acknowledge that something did not quite fit: Maupassant commented that Flaubert's language rose above the subjects it expressed, 'as though translating the motifs of poetry'; while Zola noted that all Flaubert's ideas went against 'the formula' that he and others 'derived from *Madame Bovary*'. In hatred of realism and in disillusionment with romanticism Flaubert turned to composition, the achievement of the finely cadenced sentence, the page wrought like poetry, the book as internally balanced and self-sustaining unity. Writing *Madame Bovary* was making art, not proposing some progressive sense in the way of realism, some social understanding that the reader could usefully acquire for action in the world. Where for a Champfleury a book is to be judged on its content to which form is 'inferior', for Flaubert the will is to art, not to 'reality', and the appeal to 'impersonality' is to a fundamental condition of the former, not finally to any realist–naturalist conception of a necessary stance for the meaningful presentation of the latter. Realism in Flaubert is platitude, the platitude of the reality and the platitude of this realism which is part of that reality: art alone can offer − can *be* − something else.

Sources

'the story is *entirely made up*' (18 March 1857, LdC)

Where does this reasonable book come from? Flaubert finally chose his down-to-earth subject in July 1851. It was not just, as he claimed, totally invented; on the contrary, it had a point of departure at least in a local event from the 1840s, proposed as a possibility by Bouilhet: the Delamare affair. Eugène Delamare was a health officer in a village near Rouen; married quite young to a slightly older woman who died soon after, he married again, this time a girl of seventeen, Delphine Couturier, with whom he had a daughter and who died in 1848, aged twenty-six; he himself died the following year. Such are the facts, what is known for certain, but there are accounts of Delphine having had lovers and of her having killed herself by taking poison, arsenic indeed; in addition, descriptions of Delamare, perhaps a former pupil of Flaubert's father, are suggestive of aspects of the character of Charles Bovary. The truth beyond the − slender − facts is no doubt lost for ever (there seems to have been considerable subsequent embellishment of the affair in order to make it fit the novel), but Du Camp, who in his memoirs gives an account of it that includes lovers, debts and suicide by poison, could write to Flaubert at the time of the choice of subject referring to 'the story of Mme Delamare' as being 'really good'; while Flaubert himself could worry while writing his novel that its ending was too thin, when 'in reality' it was the ending that 'held the most' (9 May 1855, B). Clearly the affair had a substance that was significant for the fiction, which does not, of course, mean that the two are to be equated, that Ry − the Delamare village − is to be identified with Yonville, and so on. In the facts as we have them we can glimpse elements of Flaubert's story − the second marriage of a health officer, the husband who dies so soon after his wife, the local Normandy setting − but then they simply bring us back to the reality Flaubert knew, the milieu that was equally his. The affair was a catalyst, the rest was, indeed, invention, the invention of reality as art. To an enquirer, Flaubert could thus reply in good faith of a literary kind: 'No. . . no model posed for me. *Madame Bovary* is a pure invention. All the characters in the book are completely imagined; Yonville-l'Abbaye itself *does not exist*, nor does the river Rieulle, etc. Not that this stops people here in Normandy seeking to discover in my novel a host of allusions. Had I gone in for them, my portraits would have less likeness, because I would have had particular people in sight where I wanted, on the contrary, to reproduce types' (4 June 1857, Emile Cailteaux).

The Delamare affair is not the only matter of fact that can be adduced in connection with *Madame Bovary*. A Mademoiselle de Bovery was implicated in adultery and the death by poisoning of a chemist's wife in 1844 in Buchy, another Normandy village, not far from Ry. The link to *Madame Bovary* was suggested by a Rouen newspaper at the time of the novel's publication and Flaubert had perhaps had something of this affair too somewhere in mind (Buchy is mentioned in passing, III, 6). As perhaps again he had had something of yet another affair, not local this time but widely reported, that of a woman who in 1837 poisoned her husband and children in order to go off with her lover and who, on receiving a letter from him ending the liaison, poisoned herself. The memory of this affair indeed can hardly be doubted since Flaubert had already written a version of it as *Passion et vertu* in the very same year it happened, producing something at least of what would later be taken up in *Madame Bovary* by making the woman the central perspective and stressing the prosaicness of her marriage. Then there was the celebrated case of Madame Lafarge who poisoned her husband with arsenic in 1840 and whose *Mémoires* Colet was advising Flaubert to read a few months after the start of *Madame Bovary*; yet Emma commits no such crime and the *Mémoires* came, if they did, too late. We drift into the realm of vague echoes, vague parallels, the fabrication of possible raw materials.

There is, however, a further source, the most striking and the most directly documented: the story of Louise Pradier. Louise was the wife of James Pradier, a well-known sculptor of the period in whose studio Flaubert met Colet. She was free in love (Flaubert himself became one of her many lovers in 1847) and freer still with money, spending exorbitantly until finally provoking her husband to obtain a legal separation. Louise's story is told by a close woman acquaintance in an extraordinary manuscript entitled *Mémoires de Madame Ludovica*, written in all probability in 1848 and owned by Flaubert who may well have been instrumental in having it

written in the first place. The study of Louise had early interested him (she as 'the type of the woman with all her in-
stincts, an orchestra of female emotions', 7 March 1847, C)
and the *Mémoires* have been marked and underlined by him
in various places. While one or two phrases in *Madame Bovary*
seem to have been prompted by the manuscript, it is above all
the financial imbroglio in which Louise entraps herself and her
efforts to keep herself afloat and undiscovered, that gave
Flaubert material: Louise, like Emma, acquires a procuration,
forges her husband's signature, sells a property belonging to
him, has to deal with bailiffs, turns to past lovers for help and
is refused. At the same time, it must be remembered that this
material concerns the life of a Parisian artist's wife, is some
way from the story of Emma as the wife of a health officer
in Yonville-l'Abbaye.

These stories of women had their importance for Flaubert
– 'it is such things one must study when one wants to write
a novel' (5 December 1846, C) – but only in so far as they
fitted with his imagination and its literary context; they entered
into his subject, a subject conceived and written from himself,
his reading, his desire, as well as from his idea of art. 'I have
put nothing in it of my feelings or my life' (18 March 1857,
LdC); but then, 'Madame Bovary, c'est moi! D'après moi'
('Madame Bovary is me! From me', the famous statement
reported by Amélie Bosquet, another correspondent). Cutting
himself off from *La Tentation*, moving into the realm of the
reasonable, the provincial scene, the study in manners, the
typical woman, Flaubert came back nevertheless to the same:
Saint Antoine was me, Emma too.

Late in 1850, his travels in the Orient drawing towards their
close, Flaubert had three subjects, 'perhaps one and the same,
which bothers me considerably': '(1) *Don Juan, one night*, which
I thought of in quarantine at Rhodes; (2) the story of *Anubis*,
the woman who wants to be fucked by God. . . (3) my Flemish
novel about the young girl who dies virgin and mystical with
her father and mother, in a small provincial town, at the bottom of a garden planted with cabbages and fruit-trees, beside

a little stream. . . In the first, insatiable love in the two forms, earthly love and mystical love. In the second, same story, only with fucking, and the earthly love is less exalted because more precise. In the third, they are combined in the same person, and one leads to the other; my heroine only dies of religious masturbation after having indulged in digital masturbation' (14 November 1850, B). He begins with the first, working on it into 1851, producing a detailed plan; something of the second is taken up in 1857 with *Salammbô*; in between, the third becomes *Madame Bovary* by a process of which Flaubert gives a glimpse in a letter after its publication (the change in recipient, from his old friend Bouilhet to a respectable female correspondent, Mlle Leroyer de Chantepie, explains the now bowdlerised account of the original subject): 'The first idea I had was to make [the heroine] a virgin living in the heart of the provinces, growing old in sorrow and so reaching the final stages of mysticism and of *imagined* passion. From this first plan I kept all the surrounds (scenery and characters, rather gloomy), the colour in short. Only, to make the story more comprehensible and amusing, in the good sense of the term, I invented a more human heroine, the kind of woman one meets more often' (30 March 1857). The Delamare affair, the subject given by Bouilhet, is grafted onto the initial Flemish novel idea, focused in the story of Emma Bovary (the name Flaubert had already found for the initial heroine; it was to her that he would have been referring when, according to Du Camp, he suddenly exclaimed while travelling down the Nile: 'I'll call her Emma Bovary!').

What is at stake in this initial conception of the subject is insatiable love: mystical and earthly love in the same person, the young virgin who then becomes Emma Bovary who herself in her way seeks fulfilment from both. Flaubert's early writings are themselves insatiably full of these varieties of love, 'the softness of a woman's white arms' next to 'the voluptuous delights of believing in paradise', hours spent dreaming of 'long embraces' modulating into the urge 'to be a mystic' (*SNPI*, 22–3). The reasonable book, that is, takes up the whole Flaubertian imagination and aspiration of desire, together with the recognition of the monotonous uniformity of existence, of the gap between what should be and what is and can be; simply, it does so in a form that is impersonal, at a distance, from above; and does so too through the representation of the passion of a woman, flatly caught up in provincial adultery. Here again, the down-to-earth subject comes out of the early writings, renews with what had already been a chosen theme. The first *Education sentimentale*, for instance, has the wife who flees boredom into adultery and the account of the subsequent recoil of the lover with whom she flees (Henry, like Léon with Emma, finds her overwhelming, grows disgusted). It also includes an anticipatory page on a woman married to a village doctor by whom she is adored and whom she is leading to ruin: 'She pitilessly devours all he earns; the poor man gets tired and dirty, knocks himself out along the highways and byways, while Madame, at home by a great fire, in an exquisite armchair, reads the latest novel' (*OC* I, 371).

To write of provincial life was to write in the wake of Balzac through whose novels it had been made significantly available as a subject, and *Madame Bovary* indeed has strong links with those novels, notably *La Muse du département* (1843), the story of a 'superior woman' bored with provincial life (but there are striking differences: Dinah, Balzac's heroine, achieves a social situation in her province, marries a husband with money, goes off to Paris to be with her journalist lover, finally returning to her husband; and then again some fascinating intertextual echoes and variations: Dinah's priest advises her to write poems in order to sublimate her bad thoughts and boredom, where Bournisien can only recommend that Emma drink tea, leaving her to her adultery, which in fact is the result for Dinah too, since her literary success exacerbates her idea of the limitations of her life; Dinah's first poem contains 'a magnificent description of Rouen, where she had never been', with the emphasis on it as the industrial city it was but as which it is barely present in their novel for Flaubert and Emma, both of whom very much had been there). Flaubert re-reads *Eugénie Grandet* (1833) during the writing of *Madame Bovary* and comes across other Balzac novels in which he finds similarities with his own ('my mother showed me. . . in Balzac's *Le Médecin de campagne* [1833] the *same scene* as in my *Bovary*: a visit to a wet-nurse. . . one could believe I copied it, if my page were not infinitely better written, without boasting', 27 December 1852, C). The influence, however, is not in this or that detail or scene or development, echoes notwithstanding (thus he claims, for example, never to have read *Le Médecin*), but more generally in the overall novelistic perception of provincial life Balzac provides. *Eugénie Grandet*, 'a bourgeois tragedy', the story of the pure and beautiful daughter of a rich miser in a small provincial town, whose life after a thwarted passion ends in a loveless marriage followed by a widowhood of good works, was set by Balzac in his 'preamble' to the first editions in terms which can be readily carried over to *Madame Bovary*, those of 'la constante monotonie des mœurs', the constant monotony of life in the provinces, and of 'les drames dans le silence', the silent dramas that are played out there. We must remember too the importance of debt and financial machination as a literary subject in Balzac (Louise Pradier is already a fully Balzacian figure in this respect, available, as it were, through Balzac's novels as well as through the *Mémoires*).

Balzac depends on and helps to create a whole popular literature which informs the subject of Flaubert's novel. Central here is the genre of the *physiologie*, that gained great popularity in the early 1840s. 'Physiologies' were shortish studies − sketches − of characters or types from contemporary life, giving a humorous 'natural history' of social mores (Flaubert wrote one while at school on the type of the clerk, 'Une leçon d'histoire naturelle, genre commis'). They were often accompanied by an illustration and brought out in collections (one great example was the significantly titled *Les Français peints par eux-mêmes, encyclopédie morale du dix-neuvième siècle*, which appeared in nine volumes from 1840 to 1842). Balzac himself published an extended *Physiologie du mariage* (1829), describing the successive phases of matrimonial life according to a logic and with details that can be traced through into *Madame Bovary*. One of the major organising principles of collections of physiologies

was the opposition Parisian/provincial life: 'France in the nineteenth century is split between two great zones: Paris and the
provinces; the provinces jealous of Paris, Paris thinking of the
provinces only as a source of money for itself', wrote Balzac
in 'La Femme de province', a contribution to *Les Français
peints* subsequently incorporated into *La Muse du département*.
Everything *Madame Bovary* owes to this physiological
literature can be readily grasped if we look beyond Balzac to
the overall production of which he is a part, to the work of,
say, Frédéric Soulié, a highly popular novelist of the time (one
of whose books, *Les Mémoires du Diable* (1837–8), has been
suggested as a source for the creation of the *Garçon*). Here
are some passages from Soulié's 'L'âme méconnue', another
contribution to *Les Français peints*:

The thoughts of the misunderstood soul fly from the lowest regions
of illegal affections to the most ethereal regions of dreams of mystical
love.

The husband remains wooden while she reads Lamartine; he snores
in bed while, next to him, she lies awake dreaming.

It is the whole of the past she has sacrificed and lost for him that
she must avenge, and the husband owes her, in sufferings she inflicts,
all the ineffable joys of a heavenly love that he has failed to provide.

The representation of the marriage of Emma and Charles is
evident enough in all this, and evident enough again if we then
come back to Balzac's 'La Femme de province':

If in the provinces there is nothing superior about the husbands,
there is even less about the single men around. Thus it is that when
the provincial woman commits her little fault, she always falls for
some supposed fine figure of a man or some local dandy, for some
fellow who wears gloves and is accounted good on horseback. At the
bottom of her heart, however, she knows that her desires are pursuing
a more or less well-dressed commonplace.

There is nothing so dangerous as the affections of a provincial
woman. She compares, studies, reflects, dreams, does not give up her
dream, continues to think of the one she loves when he no longer thinks
of her.

Deep despair or stupid resignation, the one or the other, there is
no other choice, that is the foundation on which the life of the provincial woman rests.

The Delamare affair, that is, was already a literary subject for Flaubert, as well as one with a particular closeness to him, to the feelings and themes and vision of things expressed in his early writings, themselves anyway steeped in the century's terms, in its literature. From the lyrical boundlessness of *La Tentation* to the sensible, physiological, realist *Madame Bovary* was a break with, but then also a reworking of, what had gone before.

Publication

'If I publish (which I doubt)' (17 January 1852, EC)

There is in Flaubert a declared hostility to publication, the very idea produces rage and disgust: 'If the emperor tomorrow were to put an end to printing, I'd go to Paris on my knees and kiss his arse in gratitude' (2 July 1853, C). To publish is to lower oneself and one's work, to give up being an artist. Even as *Madame Bovary* is being sent off to appear in sections in the *Revue de Paris*, Flaubert is castigating himself for his foolishness in doing like others and wanting to publish. With publication in the *Revue* completed and the novel about to come out in book form, Flaubert can still only sorrowfully acknowledge his weakness: 'How I regret having published it' (11 February 1857, Frédéric Baudry).

The determining factor in this recoil from 'typography' was the development in the first half of the nineteenth century of what Sainte-Beuve, in an essay entitled 'De la littérature in-dustrielle' (1839), described as 'the invasion of literary democracy'; what we might call the growth of the reading public, a result of the extension of literacy coupled with the introduction of cheap, rapid means of printing and the widen-ing distribution and sale of printed material – 'industrial literature' indeed. The novel was the key literary form here (though to what extent it *was* a *literary* form was precisely a matter of dispute): new, linked in its decisive emergence to the developing middle classes, not dependent for its reading on acquired high cultural knowledge and skills, it was, unsur-prisingly, the most popular genre of the time. Its popularity, moreover, was sustained by and reflected in the serial publication of fiction in the daily press, as in weekly magazines and monthly journals, putting the writer–novelist into relation with a sizeable, fairly diverse, largely anonymous mass — the 'public' (in social character this reading public was broadly middle class, but extended into areas of the working class and included a very substantial number of women). Evidently that relation was directly commercial, placing writing firmly in the market-place, obedient to the laws of supply and demand, produced to the rhythm of the contracted episode or volume, so much text to feed the presses. Publishing had become a fully capitalist enterprise, with the manufacture of novels like that of soap or any other commodity, something that numerous contemporary observers and critics disparagingly emphasised. Evidently again that relation was also directly popular, connecting the writer to a public to be captured, held, renewed, a connection that Flaubert could only abhor: 'Doing art to earn money, flattering the public, churning out jovial or lugubrious buffoonery with an eye to making a stir or raking it in, that is the most vile of prostitutions' (8 April 1851, mother).

The publication and success of *Madame Bovary* do not mean that Flaubert was a popular novelist. Nothing he wrote had the kind of success of the best-selling serials, the *romans-feuilletons* (the term and the phenomenon date from the 1830s, with the publication of Balzac's *La Vieille Fille* in the daily newspaper *La Presse* in 1836 marking the decisive beginning): Flaubert was not Dickens, let alone the hugely popular G. W. M. Reynolds, to take English examples from the period. The publication of *Madame Bovary* in sections was as a specified literary offering in a smallish-circulation cultural review and the success of the novel in book form, after the publicity from the trial, can be seen as relative even when looked at alongside that of other novels of the time with which it might reasonably be compared: *Fanny* by Ernest Feydeau, a friend of Flaubert's, published in 1858 with adultery again as its theme, had gone through seventeen editions by the end of the following year. Moreover, Flaubert's whole mode of composition was divorced from the real terms of commercial production (was precisely composition, not production): where Balzac wrote at speed for a living, Flaubert wrote slowly for art, living from a private income derived from inherited wealth. In the period of Flaubert's solitary writing of the one work, from 1851 to 1856, Alexandre Dumas produced more than twenty-five novels and historical sagas alone, using collaborators, publishing in newspapers, signing contracts for payment by the line. Moreover again, this divorce from commercial production is, of course, fundamental to Flaubert's definition of his writing: literature *is* this refusal of the market; the excessive, time-consuming, uneconomical labour of the dedicated artist is a condition of its value.

Madame Bovary is a novel nevertheless, with adultery its commonplace subject; Flaubert's fear will then be exactly that of falling into the realm of the popular, into 'doing Paul de Kock' (a smuttily sentimental, highly successful contemporary novelist − six volumes a year − who was the epitome-figure for Flaubert's loathing; de Kock, inevitably enough, appears as a favourite author of that avatar of Emma Bovary, Molly Bloom in Joyce's *Ulysses* − 'Get another of Paul de Kock's. Nice name he has'). Flaubert's letters while writing *Madame Bovary* are scattered with scornful comments on other novelists of the time, on *Emma*'s novelists: Eugène Sue, dismissed as the author of 'crapulous novels' for one clientele, 'high society novels' for another (15–16 May 1852, C), and read by Emma after the Vaubyessard ball for his 'descriptions of furniture' (I, 9); George Sand, whose works make Flaubert 'regularly indignant for a good quarter of an hour' (30 May 1855, B), and Balzac, respected but censured for the way in which his novels have taught 'stupid admiration for a certain bourgeois immorality' (26 September 1853, C), both of whom are read by Emma for 'imaginary satisfaction of her personal cravings' (I, 9). Part of the objection to these writers is that they have assumed a social purpose, a utility of art, tried to *prove*: 'The moment you prove, you lie. God knows the beginning and the end; man the middle' (27 March 1852, C). Art has no truck with utility or proof, its truth lies not in any moral or message but in itself. The artist's commitment must be to art alone, in isolation from the age and all social movements: 'the ivory tower! the ivory tower! and nose to the stars!' (20 June 1853, C). Popularity is the vulgarisation of genius, beauty is beyond the mass, literature is sick: 'it spits, it slobbers, it covers its blisters with ointments and plasters, and has brushed its head so much it has lost its hair. It would take Christs of Art to cure this leper' (14 November 1850, B).

Flaubert, of course, publishes *Madame Bovary*; his stance of disgust at the society and its commerce of literature is itself also literary, part of a definition of art and the artist *in and for this same society*. If the isolation in Croisset is real enough, so too are its limits: Flaubert becomes a writer of his time, one with others, who similarly hold to their isolation, to the idea of 'the solitary bear's life we all lead', as Flaubert puts it to the Goncourt brothers in 1859 (note the 'we all'). Flaubert the solitary alternates periods at Croisset with periods in Paris, and he, the Goncourts, and the rest exist well enough within the society, with their dinners and salons and money and mistresses and brothels – a perfect male bourgeois world. Flaubert the bear has his entry to the social sphere of power and influence, is presented to the emperor, attends on the empress, keeps company with Princess Mathilde, cousin to the emperor. Homais in *Madame Bovary* receives the *légion d'honneur* in an ironically bitter conclusion, triumph of the bourgeois, farcical but chilling; Flaubert in 1866 will receive and accept it too, following in the footsteps of his father (1839) and his brother (1859), worthy son after all, another triumph for the family name.

The point is not that Flaubert is in bad faith (*légion d'honneur* notwithstanding, he lives a different life to that of his doctor brother, the *truly* worthy son) but that the terms of his opposition nevertheless reappear as a certain social integration, reflect his given class position. The rejection of everything as bourgeois through and through is finally an assent to the status quo, leaves the dominant class and its power intact: humanity in the nineteenth century has what it deserves, which can then only be accepted, however scornfully, like its *légion d'honneur*. The work of art is separate, beyond social utility, has its own intrinsic value; but this allows precisely for the possibility of its commodification as object to be judged and valued in respect of the work it represents, the artist's labour of style. 'L'art pour l'art' is also an acceptance of the society's terms, provides it with an appropriate version of art as 'Art', admissible just because of the declared separateness and the denial of social purpose. Art becomes value by virtue of its uselessness, a luxury of decoration, a fetishism of style. Roland Barthes well describes this 'flaubertisation of writing' (Flaubert, supreme figure of the writer–artist, giving his name to the general development): 'Labour as value replaces somewhat genius as value; there is a kind of ostentatious claim to labour long and lovingly over the form of one's work. . . The writer provides society with a declared art, whose rules are visible to all, and in exchange society is able to accept the writer.'

Yet it is the contradictions that can be felt most powerfully in *Madame Bovary*, the indictable novel that cracks the bourgeois code. Art is value *and* critique, not in the sense of the elaboration of this or that social position, message, or whatever, but in its very distance, its refusal of perspective, its engagement with and beyond and in rage at the bourgeois reality. The ivory tower for Flaubert is not just that, not just ivory; for all the rhetoric of his declarations, he can never be satisfied with retreat merely to the fine chiselling of precious cameos of perfection, is too big for any etiolating miniaturisation of art. The polished sentences of *Madame Bovary* are a substantially corrosive documentation, a devastating account of the society. Flaubert was forever projecting vengeance, the dissection of his modern world ('to dissect is a vengeance', 18 December 1867, GS): *Madame Bovary*, *L'Education sentimentale* in both its versions, *Bouvard et Pécuchet*, plus plans for other novels on modern subjects (these alongside the alternative books of all the colour of the past, *La Tentation*, *Salammbô*, which in the end are not so much alternatives as parallels, themselves full of a violence and destruction that exceeds and comes back on the present in which, out of which, they are written). The retirement in Croisset is also an accentuation of rage, a more intense elaboration of vengeance, a whole *reaction* against the surrounding contemporary life.

It is the tensions and contradictions of art, novel, realism, style that give the specific creative force of Flaubert's work. *Madame Bovary* is art, but a novel, but a novel written in hatred of realism. Flaubert dreams of a book about nothing, nauseated at dealing in shit but, of necessity, dealing in it all the same, writing *Madame Bovary* for art and then attacked – or acclaimed – as arch-realist. Why publish? There is no relation between art and the commerce of literature: 'What does it matter to the mass, Art, poetry, style?' (20 June 1853, C). But then *Madame Bovary* is a novel, the very form of the industrial literature, with the political relation of art to age inscribed in every line – exposition, analysis, dissection, vengeance. What could Flaubert do but send the manuscript off, railing as he did so?

Madame Bovary first appeared in six fortnightly instalments in the *Revue de Paris* from 1 October to 15 December 1856. It also appeared in instalments from 9 November in a local paper, *Le Nouvelliste de Rouen*, where it was announced as 'of particular interest' to Normandy readers (!) under the title *Madame de Bovery*, an extraordinary lapsus (a deliberate error to arouse interest?) linking the novel to that still-remembered scandal of 1844 already mentioned, when the wife of a chemist in Buchy died of arsenic poisoning and her husband was arrested for the murder. The crime was bound up with his passionate relationship with the daughter of the local lord of the manor, a Mlle de Bovery, neurotic, excitable and a great reader of novels: at the trial, the lawyer for her defence, the same Jules Sénard who was subsequently to defend Flaubert and *Madame Bovary*, argued that she had been the victim of 'that modern literature in which bad taste vies with immorality'; this being much what he would argue had been demonstrated in exemplary fashion in the presentation of Emma Bovary, against the charge that Flaubert's novel was itself, on the contrary, exemplary of such literature.

The *Revue de Paris* had been founded in 1829, running until 1845 when it was merged into another periodical, *L'Artiste*. It was then launched again in 1851, amongst others by

Théophile Gautier and Maxime Du Camp. Initially the new *Revue* was strictly literary, having, as Flaubert thought, 'no political colour' (19 October 1851, Amédée Méreaux): 'Our principles in literature come down to this: absolute freedom', wrote Gautier in his introductory article for the first number. It published work by, amongst others, Baudelaire, Champfleury, Fromentin, Michelet, and offered a literary début to Flaubert's friend Bouilhet, whose long poem *Melaenis*, dedicated to Flaubert, was published there in 1851 (in a nice reciprocity, Flaubert was reader–critic–corrector to Bouilhet for *Melaenis* as Bouilhet was to Flaubert for *Madame Bovary*, itself then dedicated in return to Bouilhet).

Whatever its 'absolute freedom' in principles, the *Revue* had a clear sympathy for writers with realistic tendencies (a particular admiration was reserved for Balzac who had been a main supplier of copy for the earlier *Revue* and whose *Les Paysans* was serialised in the new one) and was keen to encourage an idea of the novel as endowed with a humanitarian social mission, meeting the challenge of industrialism by singing its achievements and urging it towards the improvement of human welfare (the writer called upon to 'manufacture social regeneration', as Flaubert scathingly put it, 30 September 1855, B). The realism of Champfleury, Duranty and their followers was seen overall as sordid and external, lacking both in adequate social–moral purpose and in ideas and style. Attention was paid to quality of writing – Sue was praised for social significance, criticised as a second-rate writer – but in a way far from Flaubert's conception of art, the *Revue* moving in fact, as he saw it, towards 'hatred of art for art's sake' (*ibid*). The *Revue*, in other words, was liberal, republican, generally progressive, and specifically committed to an idea and an ideal of literature as social vision plus 'good writing'. From around 1856, the *Revue* began to publish more immediately political articles, including veiled attacks on the government which prompted warnings from the Minister of the Interior. The October 1856 issue in which the first instalment of *Madame Bovary* appeared (it opened the issue) included pieces on Tocqueville, Germany and the Slavic countries, and Romania under Austrian occupation (by Du Camp).

The *Revue* was an inevitable context for Flaubert to choose for the publication of his novel − given the friendship with Du Camp (even if by then considerably cooler), the example of Bouilhet already published there, the journal's place on the literary scene; and one with which Flaubert's conception of art, and of himself as artist, could not but be in contradiction − given the journal's relation of literature to social mission, its politics of 'progress' and 'humanity', given its very existence as a journal, mixing literary works like *Melaenis* or *Madame Bovary* with the ephemera of contemporary reporting and political discussion. The difficulties were not long in coming. From the outset the *Revue* required changes; Du Camp, who saw the novel as 'buried beneath a heap of well-done but useless things', went so far as to propose having the manuscript shortened by 'a skilled and experienced person' at Flaubert's expense ('Gigantesque', wrote Flaubert on the back of Du Camp's letter). Laurent-Pichat, editor and proprietor, returned the manuscript covered in corrections and suggestions for cuts, most of which Flaubert refused: 'Do you think that this vile reality, whose reproduction disgusts you, doesn't turn my stomach as much as it does yours?' (2 October 1856). As this indicates, it was the realism of the book and its apparent negativeness that shocked the *Revue*. Looking back later on its publication, Louis Ulbach, the editorial secretary, wrote how he had realised that they were going to publish 'a strange and daring work, cynical in its negation, unreasonable by dint of reason, false through too many truths of detail, badly observed because, so to speak, of the crumbling of observation into little bits; without any generosity of sadness in an age of melancholy, with no vigour at a time when we were seeking to lift up hearts and make them stand high; without love when we wished to keep hate alive by the unappeased need to love!'

The literary reaction from the *Revue* was bound up too with the precariousness of its situation. For fear of scandal at a time when it was under close government scrutiny, the *Revue* suppressed the cab scene (III,1) from the fifth instalment, and then required excision of further passages from the sixth and final one. In the face of Flaubert's refusal, agreement was reached to acknowledge the deadlock: the *Revue* made three cuts (part of the last rites scene, III, 8; and two passages from the account of Homais and Bournisien watching over Emma's corpse, III, 9), while Flaubert appended a note of restrained bitterness disclaiming responsibility for the text as published and asking the reader to see in it 'only fragments, not a whole'. As for *Le Nouvelliste de Rouen*, it simply stopped publication of the novel in mid-December − 'we could not continue without making a number of cuts'.

The editors of the *Revue* were right to fear trouble, Flaubert too when he stressed the error of believing that it could be avoided by this or that cut: 'the brutal element is deep down, not on the surface' (7 December 1856, Laurent-Pichat). At the end of December 1856, Flaubert − along with Laurent-Pichat and the printer, Auguste Pillet − was charged with 'outrage to public and religious morals'. Was the target Flaubert's novel or rather the *Revue* itself? Flaubert initially held to the latter explanation: 'I'm a pretext. The aim is to demolish the *Revue de Paris*' (31 December 1856, Edmond Pagnerre); then, when attempts to stop the trial failed, he began to suspect some other cause: 'something inexplicable, some hidden zeal' (20 January 1857, RdG). No such other cause has been found, however, and it seems, straightforwardly, that the novel was indeed the object of attack, this at the same time providing a useful opportunity to damage the *Revue* under the repressive system of censorship and political–moral control established after the setting up of the Second Empire in 1852 − the same system that a few months later was to prosecute Baudelaire for the 'immorality' of his collection of poems *Les Fleurs du Mal*.

The trial was held on 29 January 1857 with the prosecution in the hands of Ernest Pinard (prosecutor too against Baudelaire) and the defence in those of Sénard. In addition to the more literary aspects of the defence, rejecting the allegations of immorality and arguing Flaubert's artistic seriousness, a great deal was made of Flaubert's social position (Sénard: 'His name is Flaubert, he is the second son of M. Flaubert'), the self-willed demoraliser of the bourgeois world presented as beyond reproach exactly because of his credentials as a bourgeois, his solid family background. The verdict delivered on 7 February was one of acquittal, the court recognising that 'a certain moral lesson' could be drawn from the novel but coupling this with 'a severe reprimand, since the mission of literature must be to embellish and refresh the mind by raising the understanding and refining morals, more than to impart disgust with vice by offering a picture of the disorders which may exist in society'. Baudelaire was to be less fortunate, condemned to a fine and the suppression of certain poems; as was the *Revue* itself, suspended for a month in January 1857 at the request of the German ambassador for an article on King Frederick William, and then banned completely by the government a year later as part of its crackdown on political opposition in the aftermath of the Orsini plot against the emperor.

The trial inevitably gave Flaubert celebrity, and his novel an assured success: 'everyone has read it, is reading it or wants to read it' (16 January 1857, brother). The rights for five years had been ceded to the publisher Michel Lévy for 800 francs just prior to the bringing of the charges. The novel was published in book form in a first printing of 6,000 copies in April 1857, in two 18° volumes (of 232 and 258 pages) with the yellowish-green cover of the 'Collection Michel Lévy'; included was an initial dedication to Sénard in gratitude for his defence at the trial ('Through your magnificent speech for the defence, my work has acquired for me an unexpected authority'). Sales were high, and Lévy quickly arranged for a second printing in June, followed by a third later in the year. A minimum of 29,000 copies were printed in the five years of the initial contract and the profit to Lévy as publisher and bookseller is estimated at some 35,000 francs. Flaubert was quickly upset at the disproportion between that profit and his own (the 800 francs plus another 500 paid as a bonus in August 1857), but Lévy's offer had been well within conventional rates for an unknown author and the trial and the publicity it would bring had not been foreseen. At the end of the five years, Lévy paid 10,000 francs for renewal of the rights and for rights to Flaubert's next novel, *Salammbô*.

Lévy, in fact, was in the forefront of the commercial book publishing of his time. The 'Collection Michel Lévy' was started in 1856 as a massive venture in cheap, quality literature, offering 'the choice of the best contemporary works' and 'the elite of contemporary authors' in editions selling at one franc the volume, often of 350–400 pages. In April 1857, the month of *Madame Bovary*, after a single year in existence, the collection numbered 211 titles across a range of genres, and included authors such as Sand, Lamartine, Nerval, Gautier, Scribe. A few years later the bachelor man-about-town hero of Elizabeth Braddon's best-selling sensation novel *Lady Audley's Secret* (1862) would have naturally amongst his possessions 'all Michel Lévy's publications', a simple enough indication of the success and renown of Flaubert's publisher.

Reception

'Nothing is missing from my triumph' (3 or 4 October 1857, JD)

The immediate critical reception of the book largely took up the terms of the trial, repeating the arguments of the prosecution speech and the warnings contained in the judgement. Indignation was common ('Art ends the moment it is invaded by filth' declared *L'Univers*, a formulation ironically close to Flaubert's own expressions of despair as to the possibilities of art in such a fetid age; in England *The Saturday Review* thought it 'one of the most revolting productions that ever issued from a novelist's brain'); much was made of brutality, lack of moral perspective, absence of feeling. An exception, and the all-important response, was provided by Sainte-Beuve in the review already mentioned that he wrote for the semi-official government paper *Le Moniteur*. Sainte-Beuve praised the art and power of the work, with its 'stern and pitiless truth', recognising in it the signs of its times: 'The work bears the imprint of the time of its publication. I am told that it was begun several years ago, but it appears at the right moment. . . For in many places and under a variety of forms, I detect signs of a new literary manner: science, observation, maturity, strength, a little harshness.' He too, however, pointed to the scabrous nature of the matter of the book ('he should absolutely not have gone so far'), and regretted the omission of any beauty or innocence, any indication of virtue ('good is too absent, no one represents it'): 'is it the true function of art to reject all consolation, to reject all clemency and gentleness for the sake of total truth?'

The review contributed much to the novel's success (Flaubert instantly fired off a letter of gratitude: 'I am covered with confusion. . . Thank you, Monsieur, thank you', 5 May 1857), guaranteeing full critical attention as critics felt called upon to pronounce on it in response to Sainte-Beuve's admiration. Significantly, the review consecrated the image for stating Flaubert's purpose in *Madame Bovary* that, however close it may seem to his own account at points of what he was doing, was to haunt him as the commonplace for its misreading, the received idea of its writing, the image of *the scalpel*: 'Son and brother of distinguished medical men, M. Gustave Flaubert handles the pen like others the scalpel. Anatomists and physiologists, I meet you at every turn!' Or, as the *Dictionnaire des idées reçues* has it, at the end of Flaubert's life, necessarily finding a place for this stereotype along with all the others: 'NOVEL   There are novels written with the point of a scalpel. E.g. *Madame Bovary*' (*BP*, 550).

Anatomists and physiologists at every turn, the signs of a new literary manner. . . Against schools, in hatred of realism, solitary artist, Flaubert nevertheless writes in *Madame Bovary* a novel that is quite generally taken as the model expression of a new contemporary literary mode. For Barbey d'Aurevilly, this was literature in the age of the machine: 'If machines were created in good English steel in Birmingham or Manchester to narrate or analyse, machines which would run all on their own thanks to some unknown laws of dynamics, they would function exactly like M. Flaubert.' Though Duranty in his little journal *Le Réalisme* objected to it along similar lines as the work of 'an arithmetician' lacking in feeling, Champfleury, the other major exponent of 'réalisme', was moved to comment with all the aplomb of satisfied self-delusion that

'*Madame Bovary* could be by me' (he had some criticisms, however, of Flaubert's lack of taste − 'a little too much surgery in the cut-off leg'). In 1858, the melodramatic novelist Jules Janin, prefacing Feydeau's *Fanny*, could stress its elegance by praising the absence from it of any realism, using *Madame Bovary* quite naturally as the reference for what that might mean: '*Realism*! Namely girls spattered with dirt, mudbaths, bibulous funerals' (Emma sinks into the fields on her early-morning visits to Rodolphe, 'the mud of their meetings', II, 12; Homais and Bournisien polish off a bottle of brandy during their wake over Emma's body, III,9). The trial itself cast its judgement as a criticism of the realist mode, denouncing a system of 'reproducing in all their departures from accepted standards the actions, words and gestures of the characters a writer has set himself to depict. . . which would lead to a realism that would be the negation of the beautiful and the good'. *Madame Bovary*, that is, became a byword for realism, 'the realist novel that has made such a stir!', as a popular stage farce, *Les Vaches landaises*, was putting it at the end of 1857 (the Emma Bovary character made her entry crying 'Save me!' and proceeded to sing a song on her marital lapses: 'It's all the same to me/I like originality/And I'm bored in Normandy').

The reception of the novel as realism had a political edge. In a long piece in *Le Correspondant*, Armand de Pontmartin linked Flaubert to the spread of democracy: 'So what is this novel . . .? We believe it can be defined in a few words: *Madame Bovary* is the unhealthy exaltation of the senses and the imagination in discontented democracy.' Flaubert, for whom the word and the reality of democracy were a matter of abhorrence, was taken to represent the democratic in literature by virtue of what was seen as an extreme refusal of 'elevation', of any ideal, and a vision of 'implacable equality'. Everything is held at the same level, with people equalised in their relentless ordinariness and their similar treat-ment: 'the kitchen-maid, the chemist's boy, the gravedigger, the beggar have an enormous place'; surroundings and things, moreover, have as much place too, described 'without love, without any preference, solely because the material objects are there, because the photographic apparatus has been set up and everything must be reproduced'. Flaubert is thus realist and revolutionary, the two as one, realism as the pursuit in and through literature of democracy and equality; in a second article a few days after the first, this time in *L'Assemblée Nationale*, Pontmartin declared *Madame Bovary* to be an explicit example of 'the revolutionary sophisms' published by the *Revue de Paris*. Flaubert's novel, in short, was grasped as the supreme expression of a literary tendency — blueprint for a school and ideology to be attacked; and the trial, again, was an immediate crystallisation of this, debating its realism, and so its (im)morality, and so its politics. Meanwhile in Croisset, Flaubert also had the local clergy raving against the book: 'Talking of success, did I tell you the priest in Canteleu is *thundering* against me. He *tears* my book out of his female parishioners's hands. . . No praise has flattered me so much. I'll have had it all: attack from the government, bawlings out from the press, and HATRED from the priests! Taieb! buono! Antika! Mameluk! "Call me Mameluk", "tell me a turban suits me!", "call me vile uncircumcised one!", "call me Giaour!", etc.' (8 October 1857, B). The outrageous end of that passage is Flaubert's joy, a written version of 'the howling dervish' performance into which he would throw himself at dinners in boisterous — and racist — ridicule, dancing and gesticulating in exuberant derision: nothing, indeed, was missing from his triumph.

Chapter 2

Madame Bovary: novel and art

Provincial manners

'Then they spoke of the mediocrity of life in the provinces'
(II,8)

The full title of Flaubert's novel is *Madame Bovary Mœurs de province*. The second half − 'provincial manners' − gives a certain code of the novel, announces a relation of this novel to the realism associated with Balzac and his influence. In the 1842 'Avant-Propos' Balzac had defined his ambition in the *Comédie Humaine* as that of writing 'the history forgotten by so many historians, that of manners [*celle des mœurs*]'' and the first and major part of the *Comédie* was to have the overall heading *Etudes de mœurs*, so many 'studies in manners' to provide 'the representation of society in all its effects'. One of the sections into which the *Etudes de mœurs* were in turn to be divided was *Scènes de la vie de province*, comprising provincial subjects of the kind to be found in *Eugénie Grandet* or *La Muse du département*, the latter characteristically seeking to bring to light, in its own words, 'one of those long and monotonous marital tragedies which would remain forever unknown did not the avid scalpel of the nineteenth century . . . go foraging into the darkest recesses of the heart'. Writing here in 1843, Balzac already has that image of the scalpel that will become, via Sainte-Beuve, the dominant image for the contemporary understanding of *Madame Bovary*: the novelist opens up social existence, explores its reality through the hidden stories of people with all their passions and dramas. By the time of *Madame Bovary*, the provinces are a specifically novelistic subject with a specifically novelistic conception − constant monotony, obscure lives, silent intensity − to which Flaubert immediately alludes: *Mœurs de province*.

This Balzacian resonance is sustained in the novel itself,

which does indeed stand as a powerful representation of provincial life in the Normandy Flaubert knew so well, a life that he is concerned to get right: 'I really have to see an agricultural show' (17–18 July 1852, B), and the next day he does, making faithful use of it for the equivalent scene in the novel (II,8). This veracity, moreover, the matter of the novel taken carefully 'from life', goes along with the aim to present 'the provincial' in its essential truth, the particular within a fundamental typicality (that wish 'to reproduce types'). Emma's story, like Eugénie's, is to have representativeness: 'Poetry is as precise as geometry. . . My poor Bovary is no doubt suffering and weeping at this very moment in twenty French villages at once' (14 August 1853, C). After the publication of the novel in the *Revue de Paris*, Flaubert received a letter from a provincial woman, Mlle Leroyer de Chantepie, claiming herself as one such Bovary and praising the novel's accuracy: 'you have written a masterpiece of naturalness and truth. . . those are indeed the ways [*les mœurs*] of the province where I was born, where I have spent my life' (Leroyer de Chantepie herself had recourse to the scalpel image, and this before Sainte-Beuve's review: 'it is the scalpel applied to the heart, the soul, the world, alas!, in all its hideousness').

'Nothing, in fact, has changed at Yonville since the events about to be recorded', announces a narrating voice, presenting Yonville-l'Abbaye just before the arrival of Charles and Emma (II,1). The writing of time in the novel reflects this: history is written into stagnation, there is a feeling of immobility that Leroyer de Chantepie catches too in the fall of 'where I was born, where I have spent my life'. One of the differences between *Madame Bovary* and a novel by Balzac is the absence of dates and other evident historical indications; indeed, from the plans and drafts to the finished novel, Flaubert tended to delete direct chronological markers, leaving a temporality of moments and seasons – 'one Sunday morning', 'during the whole winter' – and a sense of repetition and sameness rather than development and transformation. Certainly it is possible nevertheless to establish an approximate chronology: we go from Charles's studies and first marriage in the 1830s, to his marriage to Emma in 1839 (there is some argument for 1838), to her affair with Rodolphe in 1842–3 (the elopement is fixed for 'the fourth of September, a Monday', II,12, a vital detail for dating the novel's action), to her affair with Léon in 1844–6, to her death in March of that last year and the death of Charles soon after, to the final present of the narration in 1856, with Berthe Bovary in the cotton-mill and Homais receiving the *légion d'honneur*. What is then striking about this, however, apart from the gap between the detective work needed for such a reconstruction and the reader's actual awareness of time in the novel, is the avoidance in the main action of 1830 and 1848: the story of Charles and Emma is set between the July revolution and the coming to power of Louis-Philippe and the February revolution and the coming to power of Louis-Napoleon. It is as though the provincial life is held aside from the national history, which then in turn loses its significance, represents no real change; with the present narration in the 1850s — as Flaubert writes his novel — confirming this: nothing has changed. The tightly enclosed space of the novel also adds to this effect: the action is confined to a couple of villages and a town, with Paris a far-off reference, vague and imaginary, and transport restricted to coaches, horses, foot, no railway, no boats even — save the one in which Emma and Léon are rowed on their 'honeymoon' in — where else? — Rouen. Rouen itself, moreover, is given no historical recognition. The fifth French town when Flaubert was writing, it was a flourishing commercial port and the centre of the cotton industry in France, with an industrial working class and slum areas — none of which has more than the barest existence in the novel (only the visit to the half-finished mill, II,5; what Charles sees from the window of his student room, I,1; 'the noises of the town', III,3). What anyway could it signify for Flaubert but the fixed present of the bourgeois civilisation? There is no longer any *history*, and the provincial world, its cities included, figures a reality of stasis, a truth that the superficial agitation of Paris and politics merely hides as it blindly pushes forward into more of the same.

'Nothing, in fact, has changed.' But then, equally, there *has* been change: the tense of the novel is that of the stifling permanence of the bourgeois, the eternalisation of its mediocrity; its action is that of the establishment of that permanence, bourgeois progress. The monotony of provincial life has its history in these terms, shown through the shifting finances of Flaubert's characters. Though the world of the novel has its instances of stable wealth and class (the old order of the aristocracy, the Marquis d'Andervilliers; the *rentier* gentleman-farmer, Rodolphe, said to have a private income of '*at least fifteen thousand francs*', II,7), the main impression is one of mobility, money on the move, an economic and social transformation in which a truly middle class is finding itself, adjusting positions, gaining a power through commerce and small finance, with individual winners and losers in the process — Homais and Lheureux succeed, Charles fails. The central social perception of *Madame Bovary* is of exactly this *accomplishment* of the middle class and its consequent existence as all-englobing order and representation of the society it creates; the dominance of industrial and financial capital and its values is accompanied by the development of an extended middle class — the middle classes — and the general elaboration of a social–moral reason, a whole (*petit-*) bourgeois culture. Against which are the marginalised and asocial, those in misery, subject to exploitation, excluded: labourers and servants, women, the deformed — Catherine Leroux, Mère Rolet, Hippolyte, the blind man. Not surprisingly, Homais, paragon of the bourgeois and voice of (its) progress, is at once unable to cure the latter and determined to eradicate him, to put him precisely out of sight. Homais is the social mean, with the blind man its rejected excess, grotesquely close to Emma, herself a threatening disturbance to the good commerce of society, to its values and order.

It is in its depiction of the movement of social forces and the relation of that movement to money that *Madame Bovary* comes closest in its study of provincial life to the Balzacian model. It is not just that the buying and selling of things and the borrowing and lending of money are a constant activity in the novel, it is that the novel's very action is financial,

strongly determined by this activity. No less than five financial failures are presented or reported: (1) the decline of
Charles-Denis-Bartholomé Bovary, father of Charles: forced
to leave the army in which he was an assistant surgeon-major,
he marries a hosier's daughter with a large dowry on which
he proceeds to live for two or three years before going unsuc-
cessfully into manufacturing and then farming, ending in much
reduced circumstances; (2) the financial disappointment of
Charles's first wife, the widow Dubuc, selected for him by his
mother because of her reputed fortune, some of which is stolen
by her lawyer while the rest was simply a lie ('Monsieur Bovary
senior smashed a chair on the floor and accused his wife of
ruining their son', I,2); (3) the worsening fortunes of old
Rouault, Emma's father, who loses money every year on his
farm and finishes up paralysed, unable to do anything for his
granddaughter; (4) the collapse of M. Tellier, proprietor of the
Café Français, which is engineered by Lheureux (and beyond
which lies the foreseeable collapse of the widow Le François
of the *Lion d'or*, faced with competition from Lheureux's
newly established *Favorites du Commerce*, III,11); (5) the ruin
of the Bovary household: Charles has some success as an
officier de santé but the move from Tostes to Yonville is
disastrous: Homais undercuts him, and Emma's expenditure
traps them both in Lheureux's system of credit, bringing
their downfall; when Charles dies, nothing is left, 'a balance
of twelve francs seventy-five centimes which paid for
Mademoiselle Bovary's journey to her grandmother's' (*ibid*)
– Charles's father had speculated in the manufacture of cotton goods, his daughter ends as a worker in a cotton-mill.

  In counterpart to these losses in fortune are the two great
gains, those of Lheureux and Homais. The first, the happily
named merchant-draper, uses capital both as straight investment and as a means of gaining control of local commerce,
building up complex networks of debt around competitors who
are then forced to sell out. 'Everything was going well for him'
(II, 14), we are told as Emma lies ill after her abandonment
by Roldolphe and Charles signs bills and seeks loans, and by
the end of the novel everything is going even better: in

addition to the profits from his shop, he wins a good cider contract, has the promise of shares in some peat-works and, with his new coach service, is nearing the achievement of his ambition to bring 'the whole of the Yonville trade into his hands' (*ibid*). The second, the chemist, has much of the same rapacious obsequiousness and commercial cunning, putting interest over principles ('he sacrificed his dignity to the more serious interests of his business', II,11), flouting regulations (those forbidding him to practise medicine), and showing a keen sense of the new importance of publicity, of the creation of an 'image' (as witness his shop with its coloured jars and gold-lettered statements of the Homais name, its walls covered 'with inscriptions in italian, round, and copperplate script', II,1; not to mention his self-displaying pieces in the *Fanal de Rouen* and his monographs for the local academy). Just as Lheureux seeks to modernise, so too does Homais, always in the forefront with the latest commercial 'discovery': 'He was the first to bring "cho-ca" and "revalentia" into the Seine-Inférieure; he waxed enthusiastic about Pulvermacher's hydro-electric chains and wore one himself' (III,11). Just as Lheureux prospers while the Bovarys decline, so too does Homais, physically flourishing, healthily reproducing: 'Across the way, the chemist, whom everything conspired to bless, exhibited his hale and hearty brood' (*ibid*).

In this ordinary middle-class, mediocrely *petit-bourgeois* world, it is the *economy* of money that is all-important. There is none of the epic fascination with money as demonic power to be found in Balzac, nothing of the mystery of gold (unless it be, derisively, in Madame Homais's glorious vision of her spouse's chain: 'Madame Homais was entranced by the golden spiral that enveloped him; it redoubled the fervour of her feelings for this man, more swathed than a Scythian, as resplendent as one of the Magi', *ibid*), nothing of Parisian high finance (Lheureux after all is just a minor capitalist swindler, clever enough for Yonville-l'Abbaye). Money here does not *appear*, nothing much changes inasmuch as everything looks the same: 'the draper's shop still waves its two calico streamers in the wind, the chemist's foetuses, like bundles of white tinder,

go more and more rotten in their muddy alcohol' (II,1). Triumphant, Homais and Lheureux never spend, only materialise in
their goods, their commerce, its language and ideology;
Lheureux's retort to the desperate Emma, 'While I slave away
like a nigger here, you are off having a good time' (III,6) is
not merely a contemptuous (and racist) taunt; it is the reality
and value of this world, precisely its *platitude*, everything she
despises and ignores. In revolt against the general mediocrity,
her middling class, Emma inevitably opposes its economy, is
reckless, spendthrift, prodigal, anti-Madame Bovary.
Significantly enough, the two other Madame Bovarys,
Charles's mother and his first wife, join together against
Emma from the start, seeking to bring Charles back into their
regime: 'they would both be at him. . . He oughtn't to eat so
much! Why offer drinks to anyone and everyone! Sheer
pigheadedness, refusing to wear flannel!' (I,2). Mother Bovary
is continually echoing Lheureux and his 'while I slave away'
discourse: 'Do you know what your wife needs? . . . manual
work!' (II,7); which in turn is the discourse of the trial, the
prosecution reproaching Emma with her 'life of luxury'.

Charles and his father both make marriages for money that
fail. Charles's second marriage, to Emma, is for love, though
he does suppose her father to be comfortably off (the latter
gauges that Charles 'wouldn't haggle too much over the
dowry', I,3). On her side, Emma marries in the belief of all
those words 'which had seemed so beautiful in books' (I,5),
of that 'wonderful passion which had hitherto hovered above
her like a great bird of rosy plumage in the splendour of a poetic
heaven' (I,6). The Bovary household lives from Charles's
earnings as a health officer but also, increasingly, from Emma's
dowry, the small inheritance when his father dies, and loans.
Which is to say that the household lives uneconomically;
Charles's adherence to the reasonable mean – 'He said *it was
quite good enough for the country*' (I,7) – gives way, and from
the start, to Emma's extravagance, to the expenditure that in-
fringes those proper standards which his mother unfailingly
reasserts: 'She found her to have *a style above their means*;
wood, sugar, candles *went as freely as in some great house*'

(*ibid*). The style is the point, for Emma exists in and through objects; all the things she buys for herself or has bought for her or buys to give away: a map of Paris; a frilled *chemisette* with three gold buttons; little garnet-coloured slippers with ribbons; a blotting pad, writing case and penholder; a pair of big blue glass vases for the mantelpiece; an ivory workbox with a silver thimble; a rug in wool and velvet for Léon; a Gothic prayer stool; a blue cashmere dress; Italian dictionaries and a grammar; a riding habit; a horse; a handsome leg for Hippolyte and then another more everyday one; a riding whip with a silver knob, a cigar case, a scarf and a signet ring, all for Rodolphe; and so on and on, in Emma's constant passion for things − 'she groaned over the velvets she did not have' (II,5). Not to have the things is not to have the feelings they represent − unable to have a cradle with pink silk curtains, Emma loses interest in preparations for her baby; unable to 'play at a concert in a short-sleeved velvet gown, lightly caressing the keys of an Erard' (I,9), she loses interest in music − but to have the things is not to be satisfied with the expected feelings either, since any thing only and partially represents desire and cannot in itself, through possession, fulfil it − hence the restlessness and the ceaseless need to have more, spend more. 'In her desire, she confused the sensual pleasures of luxury with the joys of the heart' (*ibid.*), comments the narrating voice, close enough here to Charles's mother. But another way of putting it, the voice of the narration again, is that 'the mediocrity of her domestic life pushed her to fantasies of luxury' (II,5).

The image of this luxury, the freedom of expense as style, is aristocratic, the ball at La Vaubyessard with all its gratifications and excitements, culminating in the moment when a servant breaks some window-panes to let in air:

L'air du bal était lourd; les lampes pâlissaient. On refluait dans la salle de billard. Un domestique monta sur une chaise et cassa deux vitres; au bruit des éclats de verre, madame Bovary tourna la tête et aperçut dans le jardin, contre les carreaux, des faces de paysans qui regardaient. Alors le souvenir des Bertaux lui arriva. Elle revit la ferme, la mare bourbeuse, son père en blouse sous les pommiers, et elle se revit

elle-même, comme autrefois, écrémant avec son doigt les terrines de lait dans la laiterie. Mais, aux fulgurations de l'heure présente, sa vie passée, si nette jusqu'alors, s'évanouissait tout entière, et elle doutait presque de l'avoir vécue. Elle était là; puis autour du bal, il n'y avait plus que de l'ombre, étalée sur tout le reste. Elle mangeait alors une glace au marasquin, qu'elle tenait de la main gauche dans une co-quille de vermeil, et fermait à demi les yeux, la cuiller entre les dents.
                                                                    (I,8).

(It was stuffy in the ballroom; the lamps were growing dim. There was a general movement into the billiard-room. A servant climbed up on a chair and broke two window-panes; at the sound of the glass shattering, Madame Bovary turned and caught sight of some peasants in the garden, their faces pressed to the window, watching. She remembered Les Bertaux: she saw the farmhouse, the muddy pond, her father in his smock beneath the apple-trees, and she saw herself as she had once been, her fingers skimming cream from the great bowls of milk in the dairy. But amid the splendours of the present, her own past life, till then so clear, was vanishing entirely, and she almost doubted she had lived it. Here she was; outside of the ball, there was nothing but shadow, spread over everything else. She was eating a maraschino ice, holding it in her left hand in a silver-gilt shell, half-closing her eyes, the spoon between her teeth.)

It is an astonishing passage: Emma loses her past in the elec-tric tension − the *fulgurations*, the sudden lightning flashes − of a present which is real, here indeed she is, and at the same time unreal, this is her fantasy of where she ought to be. Real and unreal, such a present can only be the sensation of a mo-ment and an abrupt cessation of identity: her identity is *not* this, she is just Madame Bovary, farmer's daughter and wife to Charles, but then again *that* is not *her* identity either, her imagination has taken her beyond it. What the ball provokes is a concentrated immediacy of something else: eyes-closed, silver-gilt shell, ice, spoon, a freed luxuriance of being. Emma here, literally, has her head turned, shifts from where she was to where she should be, comes inside to be the object of the gaze of those who look from outside, other to the other she was (and will be) − in her view − as Madame Bovary. Press-ing their faces to the window, the peasants recall Emma's own habitual pose, 'standing with her forehead against the window', as Charles finds her at Les Bertaux (I,2). The window is the frame of Emma's dissatisfaction − what, in fact, can she ever

see from hers? — and then of her fantasy — she inside looking out beyond, seeking another life. Here, for a moment, she
is inside being looked at, finally in her true place, the fantasy
realised (hence the feeling of unreality, of loss of identity;
nothing real is left, except the moment). Of course, it cannot
last (the moment has no past, no future, *fulgurations* anyway
are themselves part of Emma's fantasies: 'She thought that love
must come all of a sudden with great thunder and flashes of
lightning [*avec de grands éclats et des fulgurations*]', II,4),
and in a complex and brilliant reversal, Flaubert has her, a page
or so later, still inside but now looking out from her bedroom
in one wing at the other windows of the château from whose
life she is once again separated:

> Emma mit un châle sur ses épaules, ouvrit la fenêtre et
> s'accouda. . .
> Le petit jour parut. Elle regarda les fenêtres du château, longue-
> ment, tâchant de deviner quelles étaient les chambres de tous ceux
> qu'elle avait remarqués la veille. Elle aurait voulu savoir leurs ex-
> istences, y pénétrer, s'y confondre.
> Mais elle grelottait de froid. Elle se déshabilla et se blottit entre
> les draps, contre Charles qui dormait.   (I,8)

> (Emma put a shawl over her shoulders, opened the window and
> leaned out. . .
> Day began to break. She looked long at the windows of the château,
> trying to guess which were the rooms of all the people she had seen
> in the course of the evening. She would have liked to know about
> their lives, to enter into them, to merge with them.
> But she was shivering with cold. She undressed and snuggled
> between the sheets against the sleeping Charles.)

No longer in the magic circle of the ball, the chance — dream
— time of her invitation running out, Emma is already what
she always was: just Madame Bovary again, her world that of
the sleeping Charles, of lawyers' clerks, tax-collectors,
merchant-drapers, at best the local gentleman. 'Here she was',
'Elle était là', but then, her moment over, 'Here she was at
Tostes', 'Elle était à Tostes' — 'tedious countryside, imbecile
petty bourgeois, mediocrity of life' (I,9).

In revolt against this mediocrity, Emma, in fact, knows only
the fantasies of her class, what she derives from its novels and
pictures, *its* imagination of luxury and 'Society', romance and
adventure. Her reproach to the men around her is that they

do not fit — how could they? — the imagined world of her desire as mediated by the books she reads: '[Charles] couldn't swim, or fence, or fire a pistol, and was unable to explain a riding term she came across in a novel one day' (I,7); Rodolphe, with his man-of-the-world airs, soft leather riding boots, and so on, is a cut above Charles but fails to bring pistols to their assignations, revealing 'a kind of coarseness' (II,10); as for Léon, he is 'incapable of heroism, weak, commonplace, more spineless than a woman, as well as parsimonious and chicken-hearted' (III,6). In revolt, Emma counters parsimoniousness, the economy of her class, with an expenditure that itself merely repeats terms from that same class: class as possession, consumption as value — Lheureux, after all, needs the Emma Bovarys, the customers for what can be marketed as 'style' and 'fashion'. Shown into Maître Guillaumin's dining-room with its porcelain stove, dubious pictures, crystal door-knobs, cactus, and so on, Emma's reaction is immediate: 'this is the sort of dining-room . . . I ought to have' (III,7). Such a version of luxury, with its fetishism of objects, characterises Emma in a specific class assumption of value (the merchant-draper consumes nothing, makes no display; the provincial notary makes precisely the display she also wants), involving, as the novel puts it, the false equation of objects, with feelings, with 'the joys of the heart'.

That last phrase has a context which puts Emma's position in another perspective:

Plus les choses, d'ailleurs, étaient voisines, plus sa pensée s'en détournait. Tout ce qui l'entourait immédiatement, campagne ennuyeuse, petits bourgeois imbéciles, médiocrité de l'existence, lui semblait une exception dans le monde, un hasard particulier où elle se trouvait prise, tandis qu'au delà s'étendait à perte de vue l'immense pays des félicités et des passions. Elle confondait, dans son désir, les sensualités du luxe avec les joies du cœur.　　　　　　　　(I,9)

(Moreover, the nearer things were to home, the more she turned her thoughts away from them. Everything that made up her immediate surroundings, tedious countryside, imbecile petty bourgeois, mediocrity of life, seemed an exception in the world, a particular piece of bad luck that had seized on her; while beyond, as far as the eye could see, ranged the vast lands of happinesses and passions. In her desire, she confused the sensual pleasures of luxury with the joys of the heart.)

The passage goes on to indicate the confusion, how for Emma 'the fevers of love and the languid tenderness of love' cannot be separated from the settings and objects that for her they necessarily entail, 'the sparkle of precious stones and shoulder-knots on servants' livery'. At the same time, however, it is not simply a comment on Emma: she may be wrong but she is also right, her perception of her immediate surroundings is that of the book as well; her aspirations mirror her class, are *petit-bourgeois*, but they also disrupt it, are in excess. Emma's romance dreams of lands of happiness and passion may be mediocre, but her desire is real, says something true against the world around her, makes her the exception.

It is significant that in the social context the book details, Emma's ruin by Lheureux does not altogether make sense. Lheureux profits from the Bovarys − Emma buys a great deal and occasionally pays, he gets a house from her cheaply, envisages a nice return from the credit he allows her and the loan he makes to Charles ('his little capital. . . would one day come back to him considerably plumper', II,14; this is Lheureux's sensuality, *his* luxury: the *plumpness* of money) − but there is something not entirely explicable about his pursuit of them to total extinction. Even if we assume that the sale after Charles's death allows him to recover all the money owed, it is still not clear that the hounding of the Bovarys to death was good business, merely a matter of more profit. Lheureux can calculate better than anyone, knows exactly what the Bovarys' resources are and how far he can profitably exploit them; his calculations here, however, are also *against* Emma, in opposition *to her*, as though she were to be destroyed no matter what, pursued as Homais pursues the blind man, also to be destroyed. Emma's fault is to give Madame Bovary a story (compare Madame Homais or Madame Tuvache, contained in their wifely role, no stories), and the story, scandalously, reflects and condemns that existing reality of imbecile petty bourgeois, monotonous and mediocre.

The novel's title is again important: *Madame Bovary Mœurs de province*. Nothing there is Emma's. *Mœurs de province* announces a social vision of the novel and a social reality, the provincial life, of which she is a part; while *Madame Bovary* states her social place, leaves her personally nameless, as Rodolphe reminds her (though as part of his own strategy of possession): 'Madame Bovary! Everybody calls you that! And it isn't your name anyway; it's someone else's' (II,9). 'Madame Bovary', or 'My wife! my wife!' (II,13): Emma is not only someone else's, she is the mere repetition of a function — the third Madame Bovary in the novel and the second wife. What existence does Emma have? Wife of Charles, lover of Rodolphe, lover of Léon, always *of*. The alternative is fantasy, being the heroine of this or that romantic novel, no alternative at all. But then Emma *is* the heroine of *this* novel, which is not called *Emma*, some romance ending in marriage, but *Madame Bovary*, beginning with the marriage (note the speed, three short chapters, with which Flaubert gets to the wedding) and telling *that* story. As Proust noted, this novel too might well have been called *L'Education sentimentale* since what it describes is indeed Emma's sentimental education. But Flaubert calls it *Madame Bovary Mœurs de province*: the description of provincial life is the story of a woman who becomes the novel's perspective on that life, forcing it to reveal its mediocrity through the scandal of her story, at the same time that the novel has her in perspective too, as heroine of this novel but also of all those other novels, she steeped in the commonplace imagination of that very same life, herself another example of the general mediocrity.

Reading

    ' "I've read everything", she said to herself' (I,9)

No one is more ordinary than Emma, firmly described and fixed in her class and social position. Born Emma Rouault, she is of relatively modest rural origins, her grandfather a shepherd, her father a small farmer whose letter with the annual turkey gives the limits of his education; though she may in adolescence drift along with the poetic meanderings of Lamartine, lyrical idealisations of nature are countered by her peasant closeness to an actual country life ('she knew the country too well', I,6). As Madame Bovary, she shares with Charles a normal *petit-bourgeois* life and can, indeed, be just the wife required: in Tostes, 'she knew how to run her household' (I,7); in Yonville, at first, 'the housewives admired her thrift, the patients her politeness, the poor her charity' (II,5). Couple this with her distinction in manner and she merits the supreme Homaisian accolade: 'She's a woman of great gifts who wouldn't be out of place as the wife of a sub-prefect' (*ibid*).

'And yet within she was all desire and rage and hatred' (*ibid*). Emma lives social dissatisfaction, the cause of which is readily enough diagnosed by both the other Madame Bovarys as education above her station: 'Mlle Rouault had been brought up at an Ursuline convent and been what is called *well-educated*' (I,2). Sénard, defending Flaubert at the trial, concurred and proposed as alternative title for the novel 'Story of the education given only too often in the provinces' (alternative titles were a feature of the trial as defence and prosecution each tried to fit the novel to their cause): 'What did M. Gustave Flaubert wish to depict? First of all, an education given to a woman above the station in which she was born, as happens, it has to be said, only too often.'

Sénard's certitudes are more than doubtful (certitude for Flaubert is synonymous with stupidity): it may have been strategic for the defence to agree with the values of the prosecution (don't worry, the novel should and does inculcate a lesson, that of the social dangers of misplaced education), but what can it mean to square *Madame Bovary* with the moral discourse of Charles's mother? Not that the latter is herself quite at one with the critique of education she proffers against Emma, with whom she does, in fact, in her past, have something of a kinship. She it was who fantasised over her son in revenge for the failure of her aspirations: 'In her loneliness, she gathered up all the fragments of her broken ambition and centred them on his young head. She dreamed of great positions, seeing him already a grown man, handsome and intelligent, settled in civil engineering or the magistrature' (I,1). Which could almost, 'civil engineering or the magistrature' aside, be Emma in her longing for a son to make up for her existence: 'She wanted a son. He would be dark and strong, and she would call him George. The thought of having a male child afforded her a kind of anticipatory revenge for all her past helplessness' (II,3). It is mother Bovary too who pushes Charles into medicine, just as Emma pushes him on, wanting him to make a name for himself with the club-foot operation, 'an undertaking that would enhance his reputation and his fortune' (II,9).

What defines this similarity between Charles's mother and Emma, leaving aside for the moment the question of the position of women, is the desire for social status on the part of sections of the middle class with no, or only small, capital in the period after the upheavals of the Revolution and the Napoleonic Wars, when the new − industrial, capitalist − society was generating powerful values of success as professional–financial 'situation', the declared respectability of social achievement. Emma's behaviour, her attention to objects, fashion, novelty, Paris, all her concern for the signs of superior status, is socially natural; Homais, after all, in his obsession with obtaining the *légion d'honneur*, is not that different to Emma, whom he even follows in apeing the ways of Paris: 'he was becoming addicted to a gay Parisian style. . . *like Madame Bovary*, his neighbour, he questioned the clerk with great curiosity about life in the capital' (III,6, my italics). The mixture of thrift and display, morality of station and work and ethic of success and advancement, social satisfaction and social envy, is exactly what characterises the *petit-bourgeois* world, the world of *Madame Bovary*, of Emma *and the others*.

Simply, the desires of the others are within (the society's) reason: Homais gets his decoration, dementedly pompous though he may be; mother Bovary could have succeeded with Charles, who could have succeeded like Homais. Charles after all is reasonable in his aspirations: 'He thought of renting a little farm in the neighbourhood that he would keep an eye on every morning on his rounds. He would save the income and put it in the savings bank; then he would buy some shares in something or other' (II,12); he dreams about his daughter and her future as Emma does about her wished-for son, but within appropriate limits, wanting Berthe to be another Emma and marry another Charles: 'a good young fellow with a solid situation; he would make her happy; it would last forever' (*ibid*). But the reasonable Charles here turns unreasonable, this novel rips that story apart; the reality is the world of Lheureux; and of Emma who, excessively, gives it a different focus, catching Charles up into her defiance of its reason, moving him to an immoderation of passion and expense on her death (the large piece of green velvet to cover the coffin finally prompts Yonville reaction: 'His friends were very much surprised at Bovary's romantic notions, and Homais went straight in to tell him: "This velvet seems to me a superfluity. And the expense. . ." ' (III,9).

Charles's 'romantic notions' come from Emma (but also from his mother who 'even taught him, on an old piano, to sing two or three sentimental songs [*deux ou trois petites romances*]', I,1). Emma and then Charles, identifying with her desire, spend too much, but the 'too much' is Emma's opposition. Nothing forces her to spend as she does; she is not one of Balzac's heroes in Paris for whom expenditure is social necessity, elegance the key to open this or that door. From the start, the time of her convent education, Emma strikes those who meet her as different, as standing out from her station (the Marquis d'Andervilliers notes 'a pretty figure and manners different from a peasant's', I,7; Léon is overwhelmed by finding himself in conversation 'with *a lady*', II,3; Rodolphe wonders 'Where can that oaf have found her?', II,7), but the spending into which she flings herself is gratuitous, disturbing, setting her apart from her lovers (humiliated, Rodolphe refuses her gifts: 'She insisted, and in the end he obeyed, thinking her tyrannical and too intrusive', II,12; Léon is aghast at 'her expensive habits' – she even wants him to steal from his employer – and comes to a conclusion worthy of Homais: 'Furthermore, he was about to become a chief clerk. It was time to be serious. Accordingly he was giving up the flute, exalted sentiments, and imagination', III,6). To profit and interest, Emma opposes waste; to bourgeois and *petit-bourgeois* life, an imagination of the aristocratic, a sense of

style and gesture, tossing her last five francs to the blind man:
'It seemed to her a fine thing to throw it away like that' (III,7;
Homais, of course, has given a *sou* and asked for change). The
seeming is all-important: Emma sees herself in the gesture,
which is made purely for the show of her. It is through such
semblances that she seeks to achieve her difference, so many
signs of what she truly is and should be recognised as being;
except that no one does so recognise her since it is all only
semblance, fantasy, romantic wishfulness. For a while,
however, she makes the signs and manages to believe in them,
conceiving herself as in a different novel to the one she is in,
and trying to match her life to what she thinks is 'done',
'fashionable'. As the *amazone*, the vision of herself in that dress
as a true representation of her class (in the sense of classiness,
the denial of her actual social position) decides her with
Rodolphe, 'the riding habit decided her' (II,9), so the *fiacre*,
the vision of herself involved in something Parisian, decides
her with Léon: ' "It's done in Paris!" And those words, with
their irresistible argument decided her' (III,1).

Charles's mother invests her son with the hopes of all she
had wanted for herself; Emma as Madame Bovary wishes for
a boy child to avenge the powerlessness she has felt. That
Flaubert focuses the bourgeois provincial world through a
woman is significant. Emma is critically alone in that world
of the novel, and alone *as a woman* in a world of men.
Alongside her, there are no other main characters who are
women: Madame Homais is a shadow, just the obedient mother
of the children of the wonderful chemist; mother Bovary is now
little more than the shocked spokeswoman for the virtues of
conventional housewifery; Félicité is only a servant and, to a
limited extent, confidante; Mother Rolet is wet-nurse and post-
box. Women are secondary, functions of husband and family,
held within motherhood and servitude. Emma's desires are
hopeless, can only return her to the confines of her class and
sex: at best she would suit as a sub-prefect's wife; at worst,
she confronts Binet, red to the roots of his hair, with her
abomination ('Women like that ought to be whipped', opines
Madame Tuvache, III,7). Emma *wants*, wants *more*, and that

force of desire is at once to be grasped generally as a fact of human being – thus the representation of Emma will give a general psychological category, *bovarysme* – and as specifically articulated from the situation of women – thus the representation *of Emma* in these terms is particularly scandalous, *she* goes on trial, *Madame Bovary* as Madame Bovary. Flaubert's critique, that is, is developed from the perspective of the ambiguous situation of women: both ideologically central, 'woman' as virtue, purity, integrity of family and society, and socially marginal, women as powerless, subordinate in a male world.

The marginalisation exacerbates desire and the social materialisation of this is *education*: Madame Homais behaves herself, is entirely her role, there is no gap between situation and consciousness; the educated Madame Bovary does not, aspiration runs beyond situation which is then *known* as mediocre. The contradiction here is that the education of women is both valued for its indication of social status – Charles is proud of Emma educated like a lady ('Possessing such a wife, Charles came to have increased esteem for himself', I,7) – and feared for the disorder it may bring, breeding ideas above station – the result in Emma's case as the good housewives of the novel are keen to point out, repeating the wisdom of the age (Balzac in his *Physiologie du mariage* declares 'a profound aversion for young ladies educated in boarding school'). With her 'good education', Emma 'knows dancing, geography, drawing, how to do tapestry work and play the piano' (I,2); in other words, nothing of use for her role, just so many *accomplishments*, but which are for her so many indications of her value, her difference, so many promptings for her desire.

In this education, particular attention is paid to Emma's reading. The convent teaches her geography and tapestry work but is first and foremost the place of reading, girls with their keepsakes, their romances, their clandestine novels, a whole atmosphere of books to excite the imagination. This is described in a chapter that Flaubert places straight after Emma's

arrival in Tostes as the new Madame Bovary. Socially established, wife of a well-liked health officer, Emma also has an
inner life that Flaubert here presents for the first time and that
is bound up with books, their images, their words. Charles's
fulfilment, 'now he possessed for life this pretty woman whom
he adored' (I,5), is the moment of Emma's lack of fulfilment,
the flaw in the transition from reading to living: 'she wondered
exactly what was meant in real life by the words "bliss", "passion", "ecstasy" which had seemed so beautiful to her in
books' (*ibid*). It is to her books that the next chapter turns,
those lent to the girls by the old maid who comes to mend the
linen:

Ce n'étaient qu'amours, amants, amantes, dames persécutées
s'évanouissant dans des pavillons solitaires, postillons qu'on tue à tous
les relais, chevaux qu'on crève à toutes les pages, forêts sombres,
troubles du cœur, serments, sanglots, larmes et baisers, nacelles au
clair de lune, rossignols dans les bosquets, *messieurs* braves comme
des lions, doux comme des agneaux, vertueux comme on ne l'est pas,
toujours bien mis, et qui pleurent comme des urnes. Pendant six mois,
à quinze ans, Emma se graissa donc les mains à cette poussière des vieux
cabinets de lecture. Avec Walter Scott, plus tard, elle s'éprit de choses
historiques, rêva bahuts, salles des gardes et ménestrels. Elle aurait voulu
vivre dans quelque vieux manoir, comme ces châtelaines au long corsage,
qui, sous le trèfle des ogives, passaient leurs jours, le coude sur la pierre
et le menton dans la main, à regarder venir du fond de la campagne un
cavalier à plume blanche qui galope sur un cheval noir. . .
   A la classe de musique, dans les romances qu'elle chantait, il n'était
question que de petits anges aux ailes d'or, de madones, de lagunes,
de gondoliers, pacifiques compositions qui lui laissaient entrevoir, à
travers la niaiserie du style et les imprudences de la note, l'attirante
fantasmagorie des réalités sentimentales. Quelques-unes de ses
camarades apportaient au couvent les keepsakes qu'elles avaient reçus
en étrennes. Il les fallait cacher, c'était une affaire; on les lisait au
dortoir. Maniant délicatement leurs belles reliures de satin, Emma fix-
ait ses regards éblouis sur le nom des auteurs inconnus qui avaient
signé, le plus souvent, comtes ou vicomtes, au bas de leurs pièces.
   Elle frémissait, en soulevant de son haleine le papier de soie des
gravures, qui se levait à demi plié et retombait doucement contre la
page. C'était, derrière la balustrade d'un balcon, un jeune homme
en court manteau qui serrait dans ses bras une jeune fille en robe
blanche, portant une aumônière à sa ceinture; ou bien les portraits
anonymes des ladies anglaises à boucles blondes, qui, sous leur
chapeau de paille rond, vous regardent avec leurs grands yeux clairs.

On en voyait d'étalées dans des voitures, glissant au milieu des parcs, où un lévrier sautait devant l'attelage que conduisaient au trot deux petits postillons en culotte blanche. D'autres, rêvant sur des sofas près d'un billet décacheté, contemplaient la lune, par la fenêtre entrouverte, à demi drapée d'un rideau noir. Les naïves, une larme sur la joue, becquetaient une tourterelle à travers les barreaux d'une cage gothique, ou, souriant la tête sur l'épaule, effeuillaient une marguerite de leurs doigts pointus, retroussés comme des souliers à la poulaine. Et vous y étiez aussi, sultans à longues pipes, pâmés sous des tonnelles, aux bras des bayadères, djiaours, sabres turcs, bonnets grecs, et vous surtout, paysages blafards des contrées dithyrambiques, qui souvent nous montrez à la fois des palmiers, des sapins, des tigres à droite, un lion à gauche, des minarets tartares à l'horizon, au premier plan des ruines romaines, puis des chameaux accroupis; − le tout encadré d'une forêt vierge bien nettoyée, et avec un grand rayon de soleil perpendiculaire tremblotant dans l'eau, où se détachent en écorchures blanches, sur un fond d'acier gris, de loin en loin, des cygnes qui nagent.   (I,6)

(They were filled solely with love, lovers, sweethearts, persecuted ladies swooning in lonely retreats, postilions killed at every stage of the journey, horses ridden to death on every page, dark forests, heartaches, vows, sobs, tears and kisses, small boats by moonlight, nightingales in groves, *gentlemen* brave as lions, gentle as lambs, virtuous as no one ever is, always well dressed, and weeping like urns. For six months, at the age of fifteen, Emma thus soiled her hands with this dusty refuse from old lending libraries. Later, with Walter Scott, she fell in love with things historical, dreamed of wooden chests, guardrooms and minstrels. She would have liked to live in some old manor-house, like those ladies in long-waisted gowns who spent their days leaning on a stone sill, chin in hand, under the trefoil of a pointed arch, watching a white-plumed knight on a black horse galloping towards them from across the distant countryside. . .

In music lessons, the ballads she sang were all about little angels with golden wings, madonnas, lagoons, gondoliers; peaceable compositions that, in spite of their inane style and precarious settings, enabled her to catch a glimpse of the alluring phantasmagoria of sentimental realities. Some of her friends brought back keepsakes given them as New Year's gifts. These had to be hidden, it was quite an undertaking; they were read in the dormitory. Delicately handling their lovely satin bindings, Emma looked with dazzled eyes at the names of the unknown authors who usually signed their pieces as 'count' or 'viscount'.

She trembled as she blew back the tissue paper from the engravings and saw it curve up and fall gently back against the page. Here behind the balustrade of a balcony was a young man in a short

cloak holding in his arms a young girl in a white dress with an alms-
purse at her belt; or there were anonymous portraits of English ladies
with fair curls, who looked out at you with their large clear eyes from
under their round straw hats. Some could be seen lolling in their carriages, gliding through parks, a greyhound bounding along ahead of
the horses, which were driven at a trot by two small postilions in white
breeches. Others, dreaming on sofas with an opened letter beside them,
gazed at the moon through a half-open window partially draped by
a black curtain. The innocent ones, a tear on their cheeks, were kiss-
ing a turtledove through the bars of a Gothic cage, or, smiling, head
on one side, were plucking the petals from a daisy with their tapered
fingers, curved at the tips like pointed slippers. And you, too, were
there, Sultans with long pipes, languishing beneath arbours in the arms
of dancing girls; as were Giaours, scimitars, fezzes; and you especially, pale landscapes of dithyrambic lands, that often show us at one
and the same time palm-trees and firs, tigers on the right, a lion to
the left, Tartar minarets on the horizon, Roman ruins in the
foreground, with kneeling camels as well; the whole framed by a well-
kept virgin forest, and with a great perpendicular sunbeam trembling
on the water, where, white scratches standing out against a steel-grey
background, swans are swimming at distant intervals.)

   Thus is Emma plunged into romance, her head filled with
tears, kisses, boats in the moonlight, young men in short cloaks,
turtledoves in Gothic cages. . . There is an evident irony:
'*gentlemen* brave as lions, gentle as lambs, virtuous as no one
ever is, always well dressed and weeping like urns'. The italicisa-
tion of 'gentlemen' at once gives Emma's involvement, this is
her reading, her perception of these novels and their world,
and pulls us away, this is quotation at a distance from that
involvement, the ironic distance that is developed for *our*
reading in the bathos of 'virtuous as no one ever is' and the
close of the sentence where dress and romantic sensibility are
on a par with virtue and bravery. The last phrase, 'et qui
pleurent comme des urnes', brings the sentence to a halt on
an image that is disingenuously appropriate: *urnes* comes with
the idea of funerary urns and supplies the requisite melancholy and emotion, but then urns themselves do not weep, are
somewhat stony, insensible things. The English versions have
trouble with this, either simply substituting an easier, more liquid comparison, 'weeping like fountains' (Norton, Penguin),
and so losing Flaubert's effect, or attempting laboriously to

write out the image, 'given to weeping with the copious fluency of stone fountains' (World's Classics), and so losing the
effect again; losing the cadence of the sentence which stops
dead on an image, set down in three short words, that is
obvious, one need barely notice it, and at the same time edged
with a comic irony, one does notice it nevertheless: Emma's
gentlemen, impossibly virtuous, are posed for us in this final
image, and her imagination with them, itself no more than this
posing, an anthology of just such images, 'weeping like urns'.

Throughout, the description of Emma's reading touches on
what is to come, contains narrative allusions and future ironies.
'*Gentlemen* brave as lions' people Emma's books but the only
lions she finds in reality are Léon and the *Lion d'or*, the
misnamed nonentity and the provincial inn where she meets
him (in a draft of this passage Flaubert had, a little too
blatantly, given 'Rodolphe' as the name of the gondolier in
the songs Emma sings). The response to Walter Scott is
remembered in the account of the evening at the opera, when
Emma's reactions to Donizetti's version of *The Bride of Lam-
mermoor* mix intense excitement still at the fictions of romantic passion with the disdain for them to which she has by then
been brought: 'she knew now the smallness of those passions
that art exaggerates' (II,15). The sentimental ballads with their
'little angels with golden wings' introduce a word that will
reverberate round Emma: Léon, who shares the same songs
(he sings 'The Guardian Angel' to perfection), casts her in their
terms, 'she was above all Angel!' (III,5); Rodolphe knows how
to draw on such language to further his seduction of her, 'Be
my friend, my sister, my angel!' (II,9); while Charles can only
concur with the inevitable banality, 'his wife was an angel'
(II,11), this at a time when Emma has already committed
adultery and is urging him to undertake the disastrous operation on Hippolyte (Emma herself provides an inadvertent deflation of such speech: 'She would say to her child: "Has your
colic gone, my angel?"', II,14).

The romanticism of Emma's imagination is a grotesque
dissociation from reality, worthless and degrading; but it is also
more than that. The point is not just that Emma is a dupe;

her songs, for all their stylistic inanity and musical imperfections, afford a glimpse of sentimental realities, 'l'attirante fantasmagorie des réalités sentimentales'. The attraction is to something illusory, the phantasmagoria, and yet there is a reality here too, a reality of feeling: what the songs stimulate is cast in forms that are banal and bathetic, but those forms do hold some substance of emotion and desire, even if, in the circle Emma cannot break, they also betray it and her, are as corrupt as the world she confronts and which produced them in the first place. The writing is distant from Emma's seduction by these forms at the same time that it is close to what is at stake for her in them, recording complicity as it responds to a pressure of memory, involving *itself* in this imagery, this reading–dreaming: 'And you, too, were there, Sultans. . . and you especially, pale landscapes. . . that often show us. . .' (it is an indication of the difficulties of the translations of *Madame Bovary* that the Penguin, World's Classics and Bantam Classics versions completely ignore this shift in address). The distance, the irony, is still there (the well-kept virgin forest), but the writing is also implicated, with the entry of a narrating voice that nostalgically recognises the power of this literature, loses itself for a moment in these images and their expression of desire. Which desire for different worlds is the very tense of Emma's mode of being, that her reading crystallises, and that this passage defines for us at the beginning of her story as Madame Bovary.

Grammatically the tense is that of the past conditional reporting Emma's longings: *elle aurait voulu* (or, using the subjunctive pluperfect for the same conditional sense, *elle eût désiré*), – 'she would have liked', for instance, 'a marriage at midnight by torchlight' (I,3) or, as here, 'to live in some old manor-house'. Turned into speech, the longings become an imperative plea: 'take me away!. . . Carry me off, I beg you' (II,12). Books suggest a reality to her that must thus exist somewhere else; which is where she wants to be, seeking to fuse reading and existence and so, in fact, losing herself in reverie and illusion. In sentiments, attitudes, dress, furniture, even the name for her dog ('Djali' after Esmeralda's goat in

Hugo's *Notre-Dame de Paris*), Emma casts herself as the heroine of a novel, incapable 'of believing in anything that did not present itself in the accepted forms' (I,7). It is the forms, the very words, that count, that are indeed the reality of the experience as fitting desire. After the ride with Rodolphe, Emma stands in front of the mirror to recite ' "I have a lover! a lover!" ' (II,9); the formula authenticates the experience and reflects the person she must feel herself to be, since the whole point is the image she can match, the story she can repeat as hers: 'She was becoming herself as though truly a part of those imaginings and realising the long reverie of her youth, as she saw herself as one of those women in love she had envied so much' (*ibid*). Rodolphe, of course, has just brutally seduced her, strategically flattering her novelistic expectations, as he will brutally abandon her, cynically concocting his farewell letter in a demonstration of the hollowness of the novels by which Emma lives, empty fictions all. For her to be recognised as romance heroine requires another reader like herself, like Léon who shares her reading and goes by the same formulae as she does: 'Besides, was she not *a woman of the world*, and a married woman! a real mistress in fact?. . . She was the woman in love of all the novels, the heroine of all the dramas, the vague "she" of all the volumes of verse' (III,5). Or, but not for her and shifting the perspective, it is to be recognised as the heroine of *this* novel, object of *our* reading and no longer subject of her own, in the mirror of her books.

The description of Emma's convent reading comes just before the account of the Vaubyessard ball which represents for Emma the realisation of what she has read and imagined for herself. Luxury, elegance, nobility, everything is there, with Emma thrilled by the old duke with his life of debauchery, duels and royal lovers ('He had lived at the Court and slept in the bed of queens!', I,8), by the world of secret letters exchanged at the drop of a fan, by her waltz in the arms of a viscount. Back in Tostes, she immediately picks up her reading again, buying a map of Paris, subscribing to fashionable magazines, studying the novels of Sue, Balzac, Sand: 'She even brought her book to the dinner-table, and turned over the pages while

Charles ate and talked' (I,9). The memory of the viscount is all-pervasive, with the books in turn informing that memory, extending its romance into a whole world of dreams, of which 'life in Paris' is one powerful version and of which one essential characteristic is the complete erasure of Emma's class (in a draft Flaubert is explicit on this – 'Pas question des bourgeois', *NV*, 225).

Madame Bovary or 'The bad use of literature'? Emma uses literature 'for its passionate excitements', seeking 'imaginary satisfactions for her personal cravings' (I,9). Think of her reading *Madame Bovary*: she reads it as she reads other novels, she is the heroine marked by beauty and distinction for higher things but beaten down, pathetically, by the mean uncomprehending world in which she finds herself. Certain critics at the time reproached Flaubert for having written just that novel, for not having sufficiently criticised Emma's reading, and so for having failed sufficiently to criticise Emma herself, as though Flaubert wrote the novel as she would have read it. The trial itself turned on this, with prosecution and defence marshalling arguments to show that Flaubert did or did not critically focus Emma and her books. What is important here is the recognition of the problem. The presentation of Emma's reading keeps its distance, but also marks a certain closeness; not least through the inclusion of the kind of direct criticism articulated by Charles's mother who berates him with the fact of his wife reading 'wicked books': 'So they decided they would prevent Emma reading novels' (II,7). If we are not to read Emma as she would read her novel, neither are we to read her as her mother-in-law does – what would it mean to take up *her* position on Emma and her reading? Most of what Emma reads is trite and her mode of reading disastrously silly, but from where exactly in the novel can we say that? Should we not, on the contrary, assent to her revolt against the mediocre world around her and recognise the value of her reading as the refusal of her oppressive life as Madame Bovary?

George Sand would later write to Flaubert that of course the healthiest part of the public had seen at once in the novel 'a hard, striking lesson administered to the woman without conscience or faith', wishing nevertheless that the lesson had been obvious for everyone, that he had shown more clearly the line to be taken. But in this medically concerned book, with its two doctors, one health officer, one retired assistant-surgeon-major and one chemist, where exactly is health? Homais the chemist has firm opinions on the matter, including where literature and reading are concerned; he who would have liked to have had fifteen minutes with Racine so as to express his admiration and put him right on some mistaken ideas; who knows the dangers − but in the right circumstances, the benefits too − of *L'Amour conjugal* (another possible title for *Madame Bovary*!), the 'infamous book' of sex advice that falls from Justin's pocket; who, man of open mind, can counsel Charles to take Emma to the opera: 'an intellectual recreation which is harmless, edifying and even sometimes good for the health' (II,14); who would certainly be able to read *Madame Bovary* properly and derive the 'hard, striking lesson' that, of course, it contains. But Homais is no more presented as a model of reading than is Charles's mother, and there is no 'of course' for Flaubert's novel, which again we must remember, despite Sand's wishful thinking, went on trial for just that, for the *uncertainty* of its reading.

'The woman without conscience or faith', says Sand. Religion, however, is itself a fundamental part of Emma's imagination, a material of images and sensations that model her feelings and desires at many points. The chapter describing her convent-school reading also describes her responsiveness to an atmosphere of religion: 'She gradually succumbed to the mystic languour exhaled by the perfumes of the altar, the coolness of the holy water and the radiance of the candles' (I,6). The drowsy voluptuousness crystallises round the imagery of celestial lover and eternal marriage, which provokes in her an 'unexpected sweetness'. As she wants to be the heroine of a novel, within the forms and with the things established by the novelistic account of love, so too she wants to be a heroine of religion, likewise attracted to its forms and things, aspiring to an imagination of sainthood, accumulating the signs of devotion: 'She bought rosaries, wore amulets; she wanted to have a reliquary set with emeralds in her room, at the head of her bed, that she might kiss it every night' (II,14). Spending for the luxury of objects accompanies religious, as it does worldly, love, the two indeed so often confused: 'When she knelt on her prayer-stool, she addressed to the Lord the same suave words she had previously murmured to her lover in the outpourings of adultery' (*ibid*). At the convent, after her abandonment by Rodolphe, on her death-bed, these are the key moments of Emma's sensation of religion. On her death-bed, climactically, she finds 'the lost voluptuousness of her first mystical flights': she thirsts for the crucifix, glues her lips to 'the body of the Man–God', with her dying strength presses on it 'the greatest kiss of love she had ever given' (III,8). Each of the religious moments is followed by some turning away: at the convent and after her recovery from Rodolphe, Emma becomes bored, the images fail to work, the identification of herself she seeks through them fails to materialise; on her death-bed, the calm apparently brought her by the sacrament is shattered by the blind man's song which prompts her to 'desperate, frenzied, atrocious' laughter and sends her into final nothingness, 'she had ceased to exist' (*ibid*).

As with Emma's reading, so too with her religion there is a distance taken on it directly by others in the novel, notably by the priest: 'he feared the very fervour of Emma's religion might end on the borders of heresy, madness even' (II,14). To counter this he orders some *healthy* reading for her, a religious literature every bit as degraded as the secular literature she consumes: 'novels of a sort, in pink bindings and sugary style, turned out by poetical seminarists or penitent blue-stockings' (*ibid*). Religion is as wretched as everything else in Emma's world, there is no reason to choose this pious reading over her stories of adultery which at least, however compromised, can suggest some form of resistance. In the scene in which, seeking spiritual guidance, she encounters Bournisien outside the church where boys waiting for their catechism lesson are rowdily at play, his uncomprehending diagnosis of her agitation is indigestion, surprised that she is consulting him rather than her husband ('surely he has prescribed something for you?', II,6). Bovary is 'doctor of bodies', Bournisien 'doctor of souls', as the latter puts it; a comfortable division of labour in which the church purveys the 'spirituality' the society needs, provides a basis for morality and social order. The material and the spiritual are, at one level, in conflict, witness the arguments between Homais and Bournisien; at another, in collusion, witness the agreement they reach at the wake over – precisely – Emma's body. Homais and Bournisien represent opposed but united sides of the bourgeois world; each has his discourse that nothing can shake, an unstoppable self-credulity, but their quarrels run along within that social solidarity, both of them concerned with social hygiene, maintaining good health against such as Emma.

Adultery

> 'How little advanced we must be, since *the whole* of morality for women consists of depriving themselves of adultery' (12 October 1871, GS)

In writing a novel of adultery, Flaubert engaged with one of the routine literary topics of his time; as Baudelaire put it in his review: 'What is the most worn out, prostituted theme of all, the tiredest of barrel organs? Adultery.' 'The whole of your infamous literature rests on adultery', declares a provincial magistrate to two young Parisians in Balzac's *La Muse du département*, and Balzac himself in a review of Alfred de Musset's *Emmeline* in 1840 was already insisting on the exhaustion of the topic: 'Misunderstood women have become ridiculous. Adultery in literature has been done to death for a while, though it still wends its way in the world.' Adultery and the novel go together, with the former giving the latter its sexual subject, providing matter for titillation. A year after *Madame Bovary*, Feydeau's highly successful *Fanny* gave an account of an adulterous passion from the point of view of the male lover, executed with maximum psychological pathos and maximum prurience – in a highly explicit scene, the lover hidden on a balcony watches the husband and wife making love inside their house.

Fanny was not brought to trial, *Madame Bovary* was, though

the coach scene, for example, is as discreet as the balcony scene
is blatant. Pinard prosecuting proposed as appropriate title for
the novel 'Story of the adulteries of a provincial woman' and
characterised the adultery in it as 'a crime against the family',
echoing the general bourgeois moral ideology for which
adultery was quickly *the* crime; in the words of Flaubert's contemporary, the social philosopher Proudhon, 'adultery is a
crime which in itself contains all the others'. The point here
is the relation of property, propriety and identity on which the
bourgeois marriage turns and which it serves to guarantee. The
wife's virtue is the condition of the patriarchal transmission
of wealth, provides the assurance of the husband's children
as *his*, and offers male identity its security: she as the husband's
possession and the reflection of his value, upholding the
established order for which he stands. The authorisation of
divorce during the Revolution in 1792 was abolished at the
beginning of the Restoration in 1816, not to be reinstated until 1884: marriage and the family are sacrosanct and women,
whose position regresses with the bourgeois tightening of the
forms of those institutions, are the sacrosanct figure of their
achievement, the linchpin of the religion and the morality they
supposedly embody with their purity (Michelet in *L'Amour*:
'Betrayal by the woman has enormous consequences which that
by the man does not'). Hence the multiplication of studies
devoted to women, 'the woman', all the disquiet as to how to
know and control her (*L'Amour* is just such a study).

The reality is that marriage is the allowed expression of the
sexual (as love) defined in terms of the function of reproduction (for the woman, motherhood as her natural role and sexual finality; for the man, the attainment of his heirs; for the
society, the renewal of its middle class), and that the sexual (as
desire) is also not to be contained in such a version of marriage,
but goes constantly beyond its limits. The representation of which
reality is precisely adultery, developed into a whole literature that
expresses fascination with the excess of the sexual together with
trepidation at the disorder it brings, its threat to the assumed
stabilities of bourgeois social identity. The novel, the decisive
form of this literature, ranging in its individual examples from

titillation to moral condemnation, takes up the contradictions of the contemporary social–sexual relations, attempting to make good the given ideological version of marriage and the family (and of 'man' and 'woman') even as these are shown in narratives of their failure. *Fanny* titillates, but adultery is made unhappy: Fanny stays with her husband and her lover is left in suicidal despair; Janin in his preface can thus recommend it to 'delicate ears' inasmuch as it stresses from the first the punishment to come. That this is an unlikely account of Feydeau's book – which wallows in eroticism – is the point: the moralising of adultery, punished or at the very least condemned, is accompanied by the indulgence in the immorality of adultery that the former allows, sanctifies. Lacking both titillation and punishment, *Madame Bovary* is prosecuted, gets a different treatment – a different reading – from *Fanny*. But then Emma's adulteries, in fact, are hardly shown as leading to happiness: she really finishes in suicide (not just despair), her body torn by pain, surely punishment enough. The problem is that the punishment is not *clear*, not clearly related to any socially valid moral perspective. Adultery here is platitude, as flatly oppressive as all the rest. There is nothing to measure it against; or rather, everything else can just as well be measured by the adultery: nothing is any better, less mediocre. So what is the point of the novel, how is it to be read? The trial turned on this question, each side trying to *settle* a reading: glorification of adultery for the prosecution, condemnation of adultery for the defence; but *Madame Bovary* does not fit any such settlement, any such reading, which again was the question for the trial.

As a young man, Flaubert had an intense, fascinated attraction to adultery (the Trouville vision of Elisa was of a 'married' woman). In the autobiographical *Novembre*, he records how the very word 'adultery' conjured up a whole poetry of desire: 'a word which seemed supremely beautiful among human words. . . An exquisite sweetness hangs vaguely over it. A singular magic fills it with perfume' (*OC* I, 257). Less than ten years later he sets Emma Bovary off on the path that will lead to the discovery 'in adultery of all the platitudes

of marriage' (III,6); and the point is not then some condemnation of adultery, but the focusing through adultery of the
general social reality in all its monotonous pettiness. Flaubert
fascinated by adultery, its romance of the woman, was also
Flaubert fascinated by adultery as the truth behind the mask
of the conventional forms: 'the marriage bed is the mask, the
adultery consummated there the truth' (*OC* I, 159). That was
written when he was sixteen, straight from the cynicism of the
Garçon: adultery is the farcical truth of the bourgeois, the gross
derision of the morality it claims. Just as he is writing the scene
in which Emma yields to Rodolphe ('I'm right in the middle
of their Fuck'), Flaubert, prompted by the sight of a much-
cuckolded husband, launches into a dizzying reflection on the
whirl of adulteries: 'Have you sometimes thought of that quan-
tity of women who have lovers, of those quantities of men who
have mistresses, of all those couples under couples? How many
lies that implies, how many manœuvrings and betrayals and
tears and sufferings! – That's where the grotesque comes
from, and the tragic too! The one and the other are just the
same mask that covers the same nothingness' (23 December
1853, C).

It is the perfume of the word, of 'adultery', with which
Emma is so taken when she repeats that she has 'a lover! a
lover!' and envisages a marvellous immensity of passion: 'she
recalled the heroines of the books she had read, and the lyric
legion of those adulterous women began to sing in her memory
with the voice of sisters charming her. She was becoming herself
as though truly a part of those imaginings and realising the
long reverie of her youth, as she saw herself as one of those
women in love she had envied so much' (II,9). Emma becomes
the heroine she wants to be, finds herself in the novels of
adultery she has read, but that heroine, those novels, do not
correspond to any reality of things; or if they do, only by
falsehood, by the fictions with which Rodolphe seduces her:
adultery in reality is no better than marriage. But nor is it any
worse (is Madame Homais to be valued over Emma?); indeed,
it is truer, it strips away pretence. Emma's reading is worth
as much as the councillor's speech at the agricultural show or

Homais's articles for the *Fanal de Rouen*; and, in fact, more, since it does at least provide something with which to refuse their stupidity.

The crux is that the novel Flaubert writes, the novel of Emma's attempt to live her novels, is itself exactly programmed as a novel of adultery and that Emma could – would – already have read her story; as, for example, in the account of 'The Adulterous Woman' by Hippolyte Lucas in *Les Français peints par eux-mêmes* (published in 1841, the year Charles and Emma move to Yonville): 'More than one weak wife in possession of a good man devoted to pleasing her, has taken to creating chimerical misfortunes so as to attain the novelistic state of the heroines of sentimental novels, and has abandoned herself to whims of the imagination which have degenerated over time into a real catastrophe for her husband'; or as in that passage quoted earlier, in the discussion of sources, from Balzac's 'La Femme de province' (it is also to be found in *La Muse du départment*), which gives a portrait of Rodolphe down to his gloves, one of the first things Emma notices when she meets him ('he had yellow gloves on', II,7): 'When the provincial woman commits her little fault, she always falls for some supposed fine figure of a man or some local dandy, for some fellow who wears gloves and is accounted good on horseback.' Like Emma, Flaubert is caught up in the literature of adultery which he repeats; but like her again, he displaces that literature even as he repeats it: where she exhausts her novels as she realises them as platitude, he exhausts the platitudes of the novel of adultery, leaving no hold for its habitual framework of reference and value, skewing its conventional knowledge and judgement of 'the adulterous woman'. What is, where is, the moral of Emma's story, of her life as Madame Bovary?

For Zola, Emma was 'adultery itself', but what is adultery for Emma the woman? Balzac in the *Physiologie du mariage* had given an answer, freedom: 'it is only with a lover that the married woman can reconquer the delicious use of her free will in love'. The young Flaubert said something similar: 'The poetry of the adulterous woman is true only because she herself is in freedom at the heart of fatality' (*OC* II, 472). Balzac's freedom, however, is so much convention, so much novel: Emma does not find freedom but more of the same, dropping from an initial elation into lassitude and hate. What she feels most is suffocating oppression, and her cry, four times repeated from her abandonment by Rodolphe to her death-bed, is 'J'étouffe!', 'I'm stifling!' There is no delicious use of free will but rather a pliant yielding, a kind of characteristic limp enervation which the word *mollesse* (and its related forms) typically describes: 'she felt limp [*molle*] and abandoned' (II,6); 'She was overcome by a sudden weakness [*une mollesse la saisit*]' (II,8); 'She tried feebly [*mollement*] to disengage herself' (II,9); appropriately enough Rodolphe, to seduce her, takes pains to wear 'de longues bottes molles' ('he thought that she would never have seen their like', *ibid*). Flaubert's idea of adultery and freedom is thus different, in freedom but at the heart of fatality. He made this statement on the poetry of the adulterous woman, in fact, with Louise Pradier in mind: Louise with her free-wheeling succession of lovers, her compulsively zany affairs and strategies that create their own fatal outcome of discovery and downfall, and that are anyway subject to the very fatality of adultery itself, the necessary truth of the bourgeois world, and to the very fatality of life itself, its fundamental meaninglessness. Emma has much of this but is also distinct from Louise (who had a life to continue, was never in danger of suicide*), is just the provincial woman–wife, Madame Bovary, with the poetry and freedom little evident. Adultery is hers and very much not hers; it follows fatally from her novels and her world (note too the use of force against her, by both Rodolphe and Léon who hustles her into the carriage), and can thus only be disillusionment, that fatality of life itself. Which leaves this novel to end in platitude and nothingness: on the one hand, Homais and his discourse, imperviously conclusive; on the other, putrefaction and death, Emma's ceasing to exist.

*Nor *statistically* was Emma: women in her class in her situation were among the least likely people to commit suicide. The point here, however, is not some flat statistical reflection, but the condensation in the figure of Madame Bovary of a whole series of elements of the social reality of Flaubert's time in relation to an intense reaction to that reality. Flaubert *creates* typicality, a new representative case.

'My science collapses before women', wrote Flaubert to Colet in 1846 (27 September); and in 1859 to Leroyer de Chantepie,
'Woman seems to me something impossible. . . an abyss that
entices and frightens me' (18 December); with *Madame Bovary*
written between these two statements. This difficulty of women
and woman was fully contemporary. The Revolution had seen
debate around – and some movement towards – the equalisation of the sexes, with a number of women's groups and
actions, such as the 'Declaration of the Rights of Women' by
Olympe de Gouge in 1792. The re-establishment of the
monarchy and the consolidation of a bourgeois social order
with Louis-Philippe, followed by the Second Empire, saw both
a reaction against proto-feminist ideas, with the confinement
of the woman as wife, the man's property, and a concomitant
concern with woman as problematic, requiring some 'science';
this in reaction to the consciousness and dissatisfactions and
demands of women in a society where ideas of freedom and
individual rights were strongly current, a modern society that
had known and knew struggles for equality. His science
collapses, woman remains impossible, but Flaubert catches up
strongly the contemporary reality in the terms of his writing
of Emma. A lower middle-class provincial woman, her horizon
is marriage and the nearest town, her reality male, her
experience that of *étouffement* with 'escape' at best adultery
(on the other side of which lies prostitution, encountered with
fear by Emma as a possible version of herself at the breakfast
following the masked ball, III,6); literate and moderately
educated for class display (her accomplishments), she is
separated in her consciousness from her actual condition, while
her aspirations run into conventional social terms – those of
fortune and higher class position.

The importance of her reading again is that it moulds this
consciousness in a way that, while itself equally conventional,
nevertheless suggests a discourse – illusory yet strong – of
freedom and revolt. This latter is then directly expressible by
Emma in gender terms, contrasting her situation as a woman
to a man's: 'A man, at least, is free; he can explore passions
and countries, overcome obstacles, taste of the most distant

pleasures. But a woman is constantly thwarted. At once inert and pliable, she has against her the weaknesses of the flesh [*les mollesses de la chair*] and the dependencies of the law. . . she is always drawn by some desire, restrained by some rule of conduct' (II,3). Taking Charles's place through the phallic procuration she obtains from him, playing the male lead in the affair with Léon, adopting male signs of dress and appearance (wearing 'a man's hat', doing her hair 'like a man's', and so on), Emma tries in vain to accede to something of men's powers and is left wanting vengeance: 'She would have liked to beat men, spit in their faces, crush them', III,7). None of which makes *Madame Bovary* a feminist novel in any modern sense (that it is indeed importantly readable within feminism, that it had its historical resonances for feminist consciousness in the nineteenth century, is another matter). Flaubert, from early on, found nothing 'very beautiful' in 'the emancipation of women' (*SNPI*, 48) and was anyway always hostile to social movements, versions of progress. Simply, he takes and defines his realism, the reality of the social world, from woman, from Emma, grasps *her* as the key point for the interrogation of that world, the demonstration of its oppressive mediocrity. His separation from Emma is then that she is contained within this mediocrity, lacks access to art which for him is the sole possibility of liberation from it all. The position of the artist writing against, outside, in the margins, is brought together with the position of the woman as different, socially marginal, and simultaneously distanced, since *she* becomes *his* figure for a writing that is *his* art. With the distance also that Flaubert, a writer of his time, thinking in terms of – repeating – so many of the stereotypes given currency in the general agitation around women and their nature, remains in its 'psychology' and echoes its morality – the novel is not tender towards Emma who is directly castigated on occasion by the narrating voice.

The literary or paraliterary examples of the general agitation are many. Balzac's *Physiologie du mariage* dissects marriage in the interests of husbands (if only Charles had read it), a sort of half-ironic, vaguely *risqué* work of practical domestic hygiene. In the years immediately following *Madame Bovary*,

Michelet, the great historian and expounder of the national conscience, published *L'Amour* (1858) and *La Femme* (1859), two works which became the subject of passionate debate. Mysticomoral considerations of woman, they sought to counter political and social disorder by establishing the essence of womanhood and recovering women's proper role. Writing from and for 'the heart', Michelet deplores Balzac's ironic humour, but it is again marriage that is all-important, the political–social–personal destiny to which women must be held, on which order depends. As he put it in *L'Amour*, 'What is woman? The illness. . . What is man? The doctor.' Outside of home and motherhood, woman inclines to madness and violence (Michelet's nightmare is of women in the Revolution leading it into the dark days of the Terror); the urgent need is to counter this disturbance of women, to treat the new outbreak of the illness they are − the nineteenth century 'will be called that of the *disorders of the womb*'. *Madame Bovary*, with its woman–scandal and husband–doctor is Flaubert's *Physiologie du mariage*, his *L'Amour* and *La Femme*; it stands alongside those works, sharing the same space of concern, worry, fascination, problematisation, study. Sharing the same space, and then differing radically nevertheless: in excess of any given social hygiene, any given science, it offers in Emma, Madame Bovary, this woman in adultery, a critically new, complex, representative figure for the modern period.

Fate

'Fate had had a hand in it' (II,11)

' "It is the fault of fate" ', says Charles when he encounters Rodolphe after Emma's death, 'the one great thing he ever said' (III,11). This great thing, however, his *grand mot*, is not really his; indeed, it is an unwitting quotation from Rodolphe himself who takes care to find a place for 'fate' in the letter by which he abandons Emma: ' "Is it my fault? God, no, no! blame only fate!" "Always an effective word", he said to himself' (II,13). So effective that he also makes use of it at the beginning of his seduction of her, whispering persuasively of 'two poor souls' who 'will meet and love, because fate demands it' (II,8). Rodolphe, of course, 'directs this fate' (III,11); but is he thereby free from it? Charles endures it, 'the fault of fate' already his explanation for the club-foot fiasco: 'Yet he had taken every precaution imaginable. Fate had had a hand in it'; but is he thereby without responsibility? 'Fate' circulates as word and idea in the novel from this character to that, implicated in their use of it, to be read in the light of their deceits and self-deceits. Fictions of 'fate' are cited and held up as such for our recognition; as, for example, at the opera when Emma is caught up for a time in Lucie's story as in a version of the 'great love' she imagined from her reading and believed she was living with Rodolphe, prompting an identification so strong that she repeats the cry she uttered when she saw him leaving Yonville: 'the lovers spoke of the flowers on their tomb, of vows, exile, fate, hopes; and when they uttered their last *adieu*, Emma gave a sharp cry' (II,15).

The fault of fate. . . Irony? Truth? Both? Fate masks manipulation, is brought out as an excuse, is the term of a whole romantic ethos of tragic destiny (the entry for 'fate' in the *Dictionnaire des idées reçues* reads 'exclusively romantic word', *BP*, 515), but it is also the acknowledgment of the inexorable, the view from above: it is fatal, the novel makes us feel, that Emma is dragged down, brought to her suicide, annihilated; fatal that Homais flourishes, expands his clientele, receives his decoration. Fate, indeed, is also a word and a perception of Flaubert's, a fatalist by deep-seated conviction: 'As for the fatalism with which you reproach me, it is anchored in me. I firmly believe in it. I deny individual freedom' (18 September 1846, C).

The critic Georges Poulet put it well: 'Balzac, novelist of the *determining*; Flaubert, novelist of the *determined*.' In Balzac there is a vital force, an energy of actions, a whole movement of exchanges, confrontations, transformations − in short, a narrative; in Flaubert, actions dwindle ('fifty pages with no event', 15 January 1853, C) and come to nothing as they are caught in cycles of repetition and held in a temporality that immobilises everything into scenes and descriptions — in short, no narrative. In both, evidently, there is a social realism, but for the former this involves a complex process of determinations in an epic of struggle, a drama of the individual and society, where for the latter it involves the unfolding of what is determined, the intractability — the boredom — of the given, society as an englobingly infinite tissue of constraining pettinesses. Flaubert's, moreover, is a realism that is beyond any idea of value in social explanation, social action, social change; his vision is an abhorrence of human existence: 'Humanity swarms on the globe like a dirty handful of lice on a vast pubis' (25 June 1853, C). 'Fate' takes up this disgust coupled with an acute experience of 'the arrangement of things' (25 October 1853, C). Flaubert is 'tormented' by his 'talent for causality' (*OC* II, 554): everything is tied together, interdependent, concatenated; nothing is random, by chance, individual. So *Madame Bovary* is written 'all in calculation', to go 'in a straight line': the young woman taken from marriage through adultery to suicide; a study in provincial manners and the fault of fate.

Adultery indeed is a powerful topic for the demonstration of fate, the necessity of things. 'The poetry of the adulterous woman is true only because she is herself in freedom at the heart of fatality', but there is more fate than poetry for Emma: 'It seemed to her that Providence was bent on pursuing her' (III,7). This is Emma's perception, to be read with suspicion in the same way as Charles's appeals to fate, but at the same time it has its truth. 'It had to be', replies Emma when asked what made her poison herself, and this again has its truth. There is a tragedy of Emma in the face of this fate; as too of Charles, whose *grand mot* also has its truth that a Rodolphe Boulanger can no more hear than he can the true feeling expressed in Emma's stereotypes (in a draft Flaubert was explicit about Rodolphe's incomprehension: 'he understood nothing of such voracious love', *NV*, 641; an explicitness he then removed so as not to upset the fine balance, the hesitation, between the pathos and bathos of Charles and his *mot*). And beyond all this, fate is the simple contingency of the human, the

inconsequentiality of our very existence (humanity just a handful of lice) which we patch over with fictions, words like 'fate'.
Charles and Emma fall into this stupidity of words, talking
of 'fate' and 'providence' and 'destiny' when the necessity of
things is merely that: a brute reality that nothing can redeem,
though the writer can turn to irony over fictions, writing his
novel impersonally, from the point of view of God, as 'superior
joke' or 'sinister farce'.

'Madame Bovary, c'est moi!'

> 'Am I not "feminine"?. . . Lesbos is my native land, I have
> its refinements and its languors'
>
> (3 December 1879, Léonie Brainne)

Writing from such a God-like point of view, Flaubert at the
same time also writes from the perspective of a woman,
Madame Bovary as Madame Bovary. Throughout the composition of the book he continually puts himself in Emma's place,
'I'll go to the ball and then go through a rainy winter which
I'll end with pregnancy' (27 March 1852, C), until the final
experience of the poisoning which made him 'be sick into my
chamber-pot' (25 September 1861, JD). It is not just with his
heroine, of course, that Flaubert identifies; his idea of impersonality is of an overall self-dissemination, 'to circulate in the
whole creation of which one is speaking': 'Today, for example, man and woman together, both lover and mistress, I rode
in a forest on an autumn afternoon under yellow leaves, and
I was the horses, the leaves, the wind, the words exchanged
and the red sun that made my people half-close their love-
drowned eyes' (23 December 1853, C). Yet it is still the identification with Emma that is decisive; it is she who is the central figure of the book and the point of its narration: 'You talk
of woman's sufferings. I am in that sphere. . . If my book is
good, it will gently excite many a feminine wound. More than
one woman will smile as she recognises herself in it. I will have
known your pains, poor unsung souls, damp with pent-up
melancholy' (1 September 1852, C). Emma, commented Henry

James, was 'an embodiment of helpless romanticism', adding at once and pointing to the closeness of character and author, 'Flaubert himself but narrowly escaped being such an embodiment.' *Madame Bovary* is the achievement of that narrow escape − by virtue of the elaboration of a writing, a strategy of the novel, the commitment to Art it exemplifies − but at a cost which it documents precisely, closely, round Emma and her *bovarysme*.

'I think. . . I was born elsewhere, for I've always had what seem like memories or intuitions of perfumed shores and blue seas' (14 November 1840, EC). Like Emma, Flaubert had known the power of reverie, imagined another existence: 'immense, insatiable desires' set against 'an atrocious boredom and incessant yawns' (*ibid*). Emma's yearning and dissatisfaction were always Flaubert's too: 'I dreamed of the sea, distant travels, loves, triumphs, all things aborted in my life − a corpse before I lived' (*OC* I, 235). The Flaubert who used to sleep with a dagger under his pillow, 'last romantic fool', might well have pleased Emma, keen that Rodolphe should bring pistols when they meet at night. But romantic impetus breaks against actual platitude; there is no place in this world for action, passion, poetry. Like the Guérin daughter Félicité once knew, Emma has 'a sort of fog in the head' (II,5), and Flaubert likewise is wrapped in fog as he writes her, 'it smells of fog' (16 January 1852, C). Already at seventeen he had written Emma's life, only as his own: 'My life, in my dreams so beautiful, so poetic, so vast, so filled with love, will be like everyone else's, monotonous, sensible, stupid. *I'll study law, be admitted* and end up living respectably as an assistant prosecutor in a small provincial town like Yvetôt or Dieppe' (24 February 1839, EC). Except that as it turns out he does not study his law, is not admitted: from reader, like Emma, same passion for 'the most burning works of the time' (*OC* I, 233), he becomes writer, better still *artist*.

In the first *Education sentimentale* Flaubert gives his *Portrait of the Artist as a Young Man*. As Joyce's Stephen Dedalus will need to choose exile, so Jules must withdraw from all the traffic and attachments of the world 'like a king who abdicates the day of his coronation' (*OC* I, 327), like Flaubert who weans himself from things until able to feel 'rich in the midst of the most absolute destitution'. What is finally learnt is that there is no place for the artist in person, that everything must be for art; to be an artist is to be committed to self-abdication, to have assumed the ascetic vocation of art. The first *Education sentimentale* itself is not art but record, a kind of cathartic writing out of the necessary education; as such it is not for publication, there is no reason in art for the display of some artist-hero (it could thus, in fact, better be compared with *Stephen Hero*, Joyce's own unpublished draft autobiographical novel). The first book of art is *Madame Bovary*, conceived and written as such, with Flaubert nowhere and everywhere, circulating throughout, in the words exchanged, the leaves, the wind, the horses, the sun. . . Yet the portrait of the artist is still there, at both the distance and the closeness of Emma; as Sartre puts it: 'Mme Bovary is Jules not drawing the conclusions Jules draws (she not an artist). More poetical than poet.'

Art is a religion; Flaubert turns to 'aesthetic mysticism': 'Let us love *in Art*, as mystics love one another *in God*, and let everything else pale before this love' (14 August 1853, C). Here again the closeness to Emma is strong even as the distance from her is developed. Emma's religious ardour is akin to that of the young Flaubert who wanted to be a mystic for the voluptuousness of 'believing in paradise' and 'drowning in waves of incense' (*SNPI*, 23). Religion offered a space for desire, for an intensity of the imagination, a superior sensuality inasmuch as it was free from the constraints of the world, from any idea of external realisation: 'I can fully understand that people who fast relish their hunger and achieve pleasure from their privations, it is a much more subtle sensualism than the other one' (*ibid*). If Flaubert continues for so long in his life with *La Tentation de Saint Antoine*, it is because for him there is just this temptation to saintly ascesis as an extravagance of desire, as expression of the desire for desire: 'I was myself Saint Antoine . . .'. In which context we can recall Flaubert's 'initial idea' for *Madame Bovary* of making its heroine 'a virgin living in the heart of the provinces, growing old in sorrow and so reaching the final stages of mysticism and of *imagined* passion' (Flaubert was to write something of this idea near the end of his life in the story of the servant Félicité in *Un Cœur simple*).

Emma is no virgin, but the same themes and emphases are taken up through her in *Madame Bovary*. From the aspiration of her desire that runs to excess in a sensualism of body and mind she can draw no resolution, find no way forward, other than death. Her impasse can then be read from the distance of a number of related perspectives: social study, the novel records the position of a provincial woman of the *petite-bourgeoisie*; psycho-physiological study, the novel endorses a certain cultural psychology of woman in explanation of the determinations and limitations of her development and behaviour (Flaubert has a whole theory of the late development of the senses in women that is explicit in the drafts: Emma's 'senses are not yet born', *NV*, 3; the marriage fails adequately to contain their power when awakened); critique, the novel presents the mediocrity of the society, a blanket stupidity that envelops Emma like everyone else, 'a woman of false poetry and false feelings' (30 March 1857, LdC). At the same time, the great Flaubertian principle that a soul is measured by the extent of its desire gives yet another perspective on Emma in this bourgeois world: Charles is without desire, for ever falling asleep, entirely and flatly satisfied; Rodolphe goes no further than an automatic pleasure, a male affair of fucking; Léon is pallidly submissive to social conventions, doing the right thing for his petty future; Homais is enraptured with himself and his red and green jars, longs for the *légion d'honneur*, lays out a lawn in the shape of the coveted cross. Emma has at least a certain dimension of desire; Flaubert *can* identify with his '*poor* Bovary', meets and creates her on their common ground of reverie and resistance, allows her something sublime (Baudelaire's word: 'In her petty environment and in the face of her narrow horizon, this woman, in fact, is a truly sublime example of her kind'). Which is what is written in *Madame Bovary* as Emma's tragedy; false poetry, false feelings, but tragic too, tragically held in a stifling immobility, a return to the same that she cannot transcend, of which she too is the repetition: 'Everything, herself included, was unbearable to her' (III,6).

Writing hysteria

'I suffer from writing and thinking in this language'
(25 June 1853, C)

In the writing of Emma, Flaubert achieved something as radical as it was scandalous: a new conception of the feminine, of woman; and this as a question of representation posed to the whole current system of making sense. Once again, it was Baudelaire who immediately recognised this when he praised Flaubert's novel as providing the great literary document of hysteria: 'Hysteria! Why should not this physiological mystery be the matter and bedrock of a literary work, this mystery that the Academy of Medicine has not yet resolved?' (Flaubert replied that Baudelaire had 'entered into the arcana of the book', 21 October 1857). Nietzsche was later to say something similar, but this time in violent reaction against what the novel revealed for him of the decadence of art, 'always a few steps from hospital': from Flaubert to Wagner, all of whose heroines 'perfectly resemble Madame Bovary', art has been plunged into full neurosis, unbridled hysteria, has become a 'hyperexcited nervous machine' given over to 'romantic tumult', 'physiological effects', 'confused agitation of the senses'.

The *Dictionnaire des sciences médicales* that dustily fills six shelves of Charles Bovary's consulting-room was used a good deal more often by Flaubert. The lengthy entry on hysteria, one of 'the genital neuroses of women' with 'its seat in the womb', reads as something of a catalogue of Emma's characteristics, herself in turn readable as a succession of symptoms − dizzy spells, nervous attacks, anxiety, feelings of suffocation, irritability, melancholia, boredom, torpor, feverish volubility, palpitations, vacancy, fog in the head. As 'physical causes', the *Dictionnaire* lists amongst others: a nervous temperament, an acute sensitivity, a flabby education ('une education molle', the word associated with Emma, the *mollesse* that overcomes her), and an ardent 'uterine system'; while as for 'moral causes', it is above all an excessive − 'burning' − imagination that most inclines a person to hysteria. Erotic readings and 'the sight of everything that inflames the senses and the imagination' must be forbidden; balls, concerts, theatrical spectacles are all particularly harmful; anything that exposes imaginative young women to 'the narrative of the intensest passions, to the seductive picture of triumphant love'. All of which brings us close to the depiction of Emma, to the perceptions of hysteria and woman on which it draws. It might be noted too how Flaubert engages in a certain ironic dialogue with the *Dictionnaire*: horse-riding is proposed by the *Dictionnaire* as useful therapeutic exercise, but appears in the novel as a strategic idea of Rodolphe's and an occasion for adultery, leaving Homais, more prudent than the *Dictionnaire*, to get it right in a way when he urges 'Be careful! Above all, be careful!' (II,9); spectacles are dangerous, but in the novel the cautious, medically protective Homais advises Charles to take Emma to the opera as a cure, 'believe me, take Madame to the show' (II,14), getting it wrong this time and himself, in fact, helping to produce another occasion for adultery.

Hysteria, the *Dictionnaire* has it, is prevalent above all in young women, appearing most frequently around the age of eighteen; with the most directly operative cure being marriage, which satisfies the uterine excitability of the hysteric and gives her the domestic fulfilment that realises her nature as woman, above all through motherhood. Flaubert offers a little case history of this in that story of Guérin's daughter: 'She was so sad, so sad. . . Her illness, it appears, was a kind of fog in the head, and the doctors could do nothing about it, neither could the priest. When she had a bad spell, she went off by herself to the sea-shore, so that the customs officer, going about his rounds, would often find her there, stretched out flat on her stomach, crying on the pebbles. Then, after her marriage, it stopped, they say' (II,5).

Dit-on, 'they say'. . . *Madame Bovary* deviates from the received idea: ' "But with me", replied Emma, "it was after

marriage that it began'' ' (*ibid*). In the terms of the *Dictionnaire*, Emma is one of those cases where 'the goal of nature'
has been achieved (she is wife − of a medical man moreover!
− and mother) but 'the heart's desires' have not been fulfilled.
What can be done? One must 'counter the delirium of passion
with the language of reason and advise an active life, travel
or some other means capable of effecting some powerful
distraction'. Which is excellent sense or, in other words, the
discourse of Homais (he who, in Larivière's pun on *sang* and
sens, has no need to worry about his thickness of sense). As
with the Guérin daughter, neither doctors nor priest can cure
Emma (Charles tries prescribing valerian drops and camphor
baths, takes her to his old teacher who prescribes a change of
air, so they move from Tostes to. . . Yonville; Bournisien proposes tea or cold water with sugar); nor can adultery; nor would
'suddenly and strongly' pulling her pubic hairs, a successful
treatment recorded by the *Dictionnaire*. So Emma finally effects her own cure, of a sort, poisoning by arsenic; which places
her in the forefront of experimental medicine in this domain:
in his important *Traité clinique et thérapeutique de l'hystérie*
of 1859, just after *Madame Bovary*, Dr Pierre Briquet proposed
arsenic as 'a treatment to be tried'. Indeed.

If, as Michelet asserts in the introduction to *L'Amour*, the
century is to be known as that of 'the disorders of the womb',
this is because revolutionary ideas, shifts in social organisa-
tion, urbanisation, the development of education and the in-
crease in literacy, extensions of democracy and new perceptions of rights, have furnished women with a context for aspirations to change and independence, at the same time that
bourgeois forms and values are being established and tightened. Emma is brought up against her social environment and
so against her situation as a woman ('a woman is constantly
thwarted'); refusing the one she refuses the other. Again, it
is not a question of feminism, of which Emma has no awareness
and for which Flaubert has no sympathy; rather, hysteria
emerges as central to the novel inasmuch as it articulates,
however inarticulately, an opposition to the society, that society
against which Emma revolts and for which Flaubert has no

sympathy either; he too is in revolt, in the margins, like a woman, hysterical.

Flaubert, in fact, does not hesitate to feel and declare himself an hysteric, from his own illness in young manhood through to his delight late in life when a doctor calls him 'an hysterical old woman' (' "Doctor", I said, "you're right" ', 1 May 1874, RdG), and this is a powerful part of his identification with Emma, as it is of the very writing of *Madame Bovary*. Is he not sick like the Guérin girl, like Emma? 'I don't know what I've got. . . the term "neurosis" is used for a variety of phenomena and the ignorance of doctors' (April 1875, RdG). Significant here is not that Flaubert probably suffered from some form of temporal-lobe epilepsy, but that self-identification as an hysteric could have been intensely felt through his own illness, with its symptoms and crises often closely resembling those of hysteria. At the time, indeed, conceptions of hysteria and epilepsy were very unclear; the two were both distinguished from and confused with each other: for the *Dictionnaire*, hysteria can degenerate into epilepsy, which is anyway the male side of hysteria. Moreover, as Flaubert brought his novel to a close, Briquet was working on an account of hysteria as a disturbance of the brain which acknowledged the existence of male hysteria while retaining the illness as especially one of women, they being more sensitive and impressionable. Flaubert's attacks furnish the material for Emma's: his 'hundred thousand images shooting up at once, like fireworks' (7 July 1853, C) provide the surge of memories and ideas in her head that come 'rushing out together like a thousand fireworks going off at once' (III,8); her attacks provoke his strongest identifications: 'as I was writing the phrase *nervous attack* . . . I felt so deeply what my little woman was experiencing that I was scared of having an attack myself' (23 December 1853, C).

But, precisely, Flaubert *writes*, has turned to Art. Emma too would like to write, buys writing materials, 'although she had no one to write to' (I,9), pours out love letters, goes on writing even after disillusionment, 'in accordance with the idea that a woman should always write to her lover' (III,6). All that we have of her writing is the one phrase '*Let no one be blamed*' (and perhaps a word, 'poisoned') from her suicide letter (III,8), exactly a dead letter, obliterated from the novel. 'She would have liked this name of Bovary, that was hers, to be illustrious, to see it displayed at booksellers', repeated in newspapers, known all over France' (I,9), but she is just a provincial wife and her dream here is for Charles who has no such ambition, and anyway the name is not really hers; and then, of course, it *will* be displayed at booksellers, known all over France and beyond, which brings us back again from Emma to Flaubert, to *his* writing, to *Madame Bovary*. Emma has no one to write to (her love letters themselves are to her own imagination, translations into fantasy: 'as she wrote, it was another man she saw, a phantom fashioned out of her most ardent memories, the finest things she had read, her most violent longings', III,6); nor has Flaubert, with his horror of the public (which his letters record in so many monologues on the isolation of the modern artist). Both confront a public space of language that is thick with stupidity, signed by Homais as its epitome of 'sense'. Emma is silent in her world, no one can hear what she is struggling to express through her conventional terms; Homais is its voluble rhetoric, 'always well supplied with phrases suited to every possible occasion' (III,8). The fragment of Emma's suicide note, the simple sincerity of her father's letters, the pathetic gesture of Charles's paper with the instructions for the funeral, are of no consequence in the face of the overwhelming mass of Homais's publications: newspaper articles, letters to the press, monographs, learned communications − 'public opinion supports him' (III,11). Homais indeed writes Emma out, has the last word on her with his (dizzily ironic) inscription for the tomb, 'Sta viator, amabilem conjugem calcas!' (*ibid*; 'Stop, traveller, a wife worthy of love lies beneath your feet'); this when Emma's own last word is a cry beyond the world of Homais and his public, a cry on its intolerable margins: 'The blind man!' (III,8).

Flaubert too is stuck with Homais; the problem indeed is stopping him having the last word, of writing free from the received orders of language. Emma runs her course, silent, provoking scandal; Flaubert writes and publishes, equally provoking scandal, outrage against family and religion, a charge levelled against both Madame Bovary the character and *Madame Bovary* the novel. Emma, woman, lives her existence in protest, as hysteria, which is the available diagnosis and explanation of her, but also the strength of her refusal; Flaubert, man, lives his existence in the retreat of writing, which is then another form of hystericalisation, underlined by all the symptoms that accompany it (the list of Emma's symptoms given earlier could be repeated for Flaubert as well). The most stupidly solidly virile of men ('a little mistress's nervous irritability' but 'the shoulders of a porter') is also pulled to a feminisation, to a margin of writing for which woman is the figure and of which the realisation of Emma is the reflection. Baudelaire again: 'it remained for the author to strip himself (as far as possible) of his sex and make himself into a woman'. But this in reverse is the virilisation of Emma, 'this bizarre androgyne houses the seductions of a virile soul within a charming feminine body'. The feminisation of Flaubert and the virilisation of Emma correspond: refusing *her* identity, the hysteric runs against the terms of her identification as woman and so is forced into terms of male identification (no others are possible in patriarchy, which holds to strictly defined and ordered man–woman identities); refusing his social order, *his* place, the male writer takes up something of *her* position, identifies with her.

In this latter half of the nineteenth century, hysteria is increasingly prevalent and has its great moment of concern and study, culminating in the work of the neurologist Charcot in Paris and then of the psychoanalyst Freud in Vienna. Charcot, who defended his *agrégation* thesis in the same year as the trial of *Madame Bovary*, sought to bring order to hysteria, this medically most undisciplined of illnesses with its riot of manifestations and symptoms, to establish its 'clinical picture': 'It is not a novel – *hysteria has its laws*.' Freud, who had studied with Charcot, received a succession of Emma Bovarys in his consulting-room, listened to them talk, related their hysteria to the history of their sexual identity, of how they came to be women; or did not, since hysteria represents a failure in achieving stable identity, with the individual then caught in an unresolved and contradictory position, identified as woman *and* man. But what *is* this identity of 'man' and 'woman' and where are women in it, why take *that* place of woman, be settled *there*? Freud listens, but hysteria also says more than he can hear, protests against that very system of 'woman'-to-'man' identity, is not just failure but also refusal to fall into its terms. Freud too wants a lawful explanation, produces a scientific account, but at the same time the case histories he records exceed his control, leaving him surprised at the way his papers seem not to fit the norms of science and turn out like novels – like *Madame Bovary* in fact, alongside which Freud's *Studies on Hysteria* needs to be read, and vice versa. Flaubert already, that is, draws on the reality of hysteria in his society and recasts through Emma and her story the discourses, notably those of medicine, that officially and reasonably control its disturbance, delimit its meaning. The original document of hysteria Baudelaire recognises in *Madame Bovary* is *necessarily* literary, the fact of a novel that can engage these questions of sexual identity and of the society which knows their urgency, of the failure of the image of the woman and of the oppressions of bourgeois subjectivity; that can engage them in a writing that runs beyond the conventions of diagnosis, assenting to none of its received ideas and moral judgements but forging instead a new version of the contemporary experience, a new social–sexual representation.

Flaubert, 'the father of realism but feminine', commented Sartre. He constrains himself to the down-to-earth subject, the bourgeois as world and material, but lives like Emma in opposition to this constraint, retreating through her into writing. *Madame Bovary* is his third and decisive attempt, and it requires, precisely, impersonality, the writer nowhere in particular, in retreat. Sartre's formulation lacks the important term: the father of realism but feminine *but artist*. The complexity of *Madame Bovary* lies in the conjunction of these elements. Flaubert takes the down-to-earth subject, skews it with Emma, and writes away from both, with no position but art. Emma offers a perspective on her world, on the down-to-earth subject, but is herself included in it, also to be seen in the perspective of that world. Flaubert's problem is his writing's inclusion too: how is one to write without being caught in the given discourses, gripped by the existing stereotypes, held to this or that position? One answer is through a strategy of copying: discourses are copied out, simply set down − Homais's speeches and articles, Emma's modes of reverie, Charles's conversation, and so on − and juxtaposed − Emma and Rodolphe's dialogue with the proceedings of the agricultural show, Homais's truth with Bournisien's, the unfolding of Léon and Emma's assignation with the lucubrations of the cathedral guide, and so on. In this way, discourses are presented in circulation and in play with one another, but no particular discursive position is taken, no one discourse assumed; the writing remains impersonal, uncommitted, other than to the work of art, the perfection of the sentences Flaubert turns.

That commitment itself, however, is subject to self-ironic deflation. 'What a crazy obsession to spend life wearing oneself out on words and sweating all day to make sentences round' (October 1847, C). The versions of this mania in *Madame Bovary* are telling. Getting sentences right is the province of Homais who performs a truly Flaubertian labour of construction: 'He had given careful thought to his sentence, had rounded, polished, balanced it; it was a masterpiece of prudence and transitions, of subtle turns and delicacy' (III,2); but the artful sentence is useless, Homais forgets it and, for once in his life, says something real: 'Your father-in-law is dead!' (*ibid*). Shaping, polishing, rounding is also the province of Binet with his lathe, working in solitude, 'publishing' nothing: 'writing a fine hand, he had a lathe at home and amused himself by turning napkin-rings with which he crammed his house, with the jealousy of an artist and the egoism of a bourgeois' (II,1). Binet's turning is characterised as a 'mediocre occupation', yet the suggestive references to art and artist are made even so, and Flaubert indeed adopts on more than one occasion the image of the lathe as expressive of his own activity: his future is 'a quire of white paper to be covered with black merely so

as not to die of boredom, as "one has a lathe in one's attic
when one lives in the country"' (15 May 1872, RdG); his
occupation is 'to make sentences, as the bourgeois make
napkin-rings' (January 1873, Marie Régnier). The derisiveness
of art is always possible: art erected as a value in this same
nineteenth century, and thus itself no more than a reflection
of the ambient mediocrity − the great writers of the past had
no need for any such mania of style and 'often write very badly'
(25 September 1852, C). Which leaves Flaubert always potentially just like Binet: 'alone in his garret, engaged in making
a copy in wood of one of those indescribable ivory carvings
composed of crescents, of spheres hollowed out one within the
other, the whole as straight as an obelisk, and of no use
whatever' (III,7). After all, Flaubert writes his novel but
Homais wins, is in control of language; after all again, Flaubert
retreats into art but Emma at least follows her desire, tries to
realise it. Hence the balance of the novel over and around her −
irony *and* feeling, the Flaubertian contradiction of art and life.

Binet's composition is straight as an obelisk, 'droit comme
un obélisque'; Flaubert's ambition is for a style whose sentences
are straight, firm, erect, muscular: 'I don't know how my
Bovary will be, but I think there won't be *one* limp sentence'
(23 February 1853, C). 'Pas une phrase molle', or, to put it
another way, no sentence like Emma, nothing of her *mollesse*.
To think of style is for Flaubert to think in sexual terms, terms
of virilisation. The letters to Louise Colet are full of examples
of the sense of this for Flaubert: to talk to her as an artist is
necessarily to talk to her 'as a man and not as a woman' (28
September 1846). His literary advice is always that she eradicate
her sex: 'pull in, constrict, confine the breasts of your heart,
let's see muscles and not a gland' (13 April 1853). The virility
of style and art opposes 'feminine tender-mania', 'consumptive lyricism', the whole currency of romanticism as
epitomised by Lamartine, a favourite author of Emma's and
Flaubert's *bête noire* of debilitating feminisation ('truth requires hairier males than M. de Lamartine', 24 April 1852, C).
The father of realism, but feminine, but artist; the latter in
terms of disengagement, impersonality, the distance to be taken

on the world and on the lyricism, the aspiration, the desire that the woman – the feminine – then comes to figure. The artist is close to her hysteria, but at the distance of his writing, the distance of his work on sentences, form, style, something real despite the falseness of the age: the impersonal hardness, at least, of art.

Impersonality

'Art, like God in space, must remain suspended in the infinite, complete in itself, independent of its producer'

(27 March 1852, C)

Flaubert had arrived at his idea of impersonality and its necessity by 1845; *Madame Bovary*, finally, was to be the novel of its achievement, and his letters at the time are full of statements as to what was at stake. 'Absorb the object in view so that it circulates in you and let it be reproduced outside, without there being any way of understanding this marvellous chemistry. . . We are to be magnifying mirrors of external truth' (6 November 1853, C). Science provides a constant reference as standard and ambition for art: 'It is time to give it, by an implacable method, the precision of the physical sciences!' (18 March 1857, LdC). Impersonality must replace exposition of the author's personality; art and its producer are distinct, as artist the writer has no right to the expression of personal opinion: inspiration, passion, emotional intensity of the self, all the romantic elevations of the poet, are the very reverse of what is involved in the realisation of a work of art – *'The less you feel a thing, the better able you are to express it as it is'* (6 July 1852, C). The author should be like God, a comparison whose most famous formulation comes just after Flaubert has criticised Balzac for appearing with opinions in his books: 'An author in his work must be like God in the universe, present everywhere and visible nowhere. Art being a second nature, the creator of that nature must operate with analogous procedures: let there be felt in every atom, every aspect, a hidden, infinite impassivity. The effect on the spectator must be a kind of amazement. How did it all come about!' (9 December 1852, C).

Important in this formulation is the idea of impersonality as realising a diffuse presence of the artist. On almost every occasion, Flaubert's statements of impersonality run into some such insistence on an all-including 'sympathy': 'The poet now is obliged to have sympathy for *everything* and *everyone*, so as to understand and describe them' (12 December 1857, LdC). The elimination of the person of the artist from the work goes along with the consummation of the power of the artist disseminated through the whole of his creation, everywhere by virtue of this sympathy: art is as a 'second nature', an equivalent to the impersonal coherence of things that is nature itself, with the artist indeed like the God of Flaubert's pantheistic vision. The hygiene of writing is not so much a matter of not feeling, but rather of not writing in person from one's own feelings and appropriating everything to them as value, in the manner of the feminine Colet or the equally feminine Lamartine. What counts is the faculty for feeling out into people and things, into the world to be recreated in the objectivity of the work, 'complete in itself', 'independent of its producer', 'suspended in the infinite': 'the artist must manage in such a way as to have posterity believe he did not live' (27 March 1852, C); the reader must be amazed by the sheer fact of the work: 'How did it all come about!, one must say, and one must feel overwhelmed, without knowing why'.

Amazement at the time of the novel's publication and after readily took the form of reaction to its amoralism. Pontmartin, who found that Flaubert had 'succeeded so well in rendering his work impersonal that there is no knowing what side he is on', noted critically that 'this wholly impersonal system' forbade the author from coming out for 'what could have protected and saved his heroine against what depraves and ruins her'. George Sand regretted a feeling of indifference: 'supreme impartiality is anti-human and a novel must above all be human'. But for Flaubert, taking sides is simply to negate truth by the reiteration of some conventional moral fiction, and what Sand calls indifference is simply the objectivity of a creation to be apprehended in its complex impartial existence. Thus he replied: 'If the reader doesn't draw from a book the morality that is there, then the reader is an imbecile, or else the book is *false* from the point of view of exactitude. For the moment a thing is True, it is good. Obscene books indeed are immoral only because they lack truth. It doesn't happen "like that" in life' (6 February 1876). Exactitude gives truth and truth is good, truly moral; proper criticism of a work is not of its morality but of its art, of its realisation of 'like-thatness', with impersonality the very condition of such art.

The conception of impersonality, therefore, has nothing to do with any idea of the development of some third person voice, some voice of knowledge *à la* Balzac, a sort of witness to things who guides our reading and decrees meanings, some supposedly God-like *narrator*. God in Flaubert's version is everywhere present but nowhere in particular, nowhere *visible*; impersonality, again, is immersion, *circulation*. It is not a question of an 'objective' position *in* the work but of a play of visions, perspectives, perceptions across the characters and their doings and their world, of a tissue of discourses, ideas, orderings of meaning; leaving the reader deprived of any given grounds as to 'what to think', not taken in hand by some privileged voice. Impersonality is accompanied by uncertainty, nothing is sure, nothing definitive. Flaubert's truth is that there is no concluding truth other than the conclusion that there is no such truth, and art is true as the recognition of that; with impersonality as its mode of recognition, against *bêtise*, the stupidity of conclusions.

Tout mentait, 'it was all lies': this is Emma's fundamental discovery one day after leaving Léon:

Un jour qu'ils s'étaient quittés de bonne heure, et qu'elle s'en revenait seule par le boulevard, elle aperçut les murs de son couvent; alors elle s'assit sur un banc, à l'ombre des ormes. Quel calme dans ce temps-là! comme elle enviait les ineffables sentiments d'amour qu'elle tâchait, d'après des livres, de se figurer!
Les premiers mois de son mariage, ses promenades à cheval dans la forêt, le Vicomte qui valsait, et Lagardy chantant, tout

repassa devant ses yeux. . . Et Léon lui parut soudain dans le même
éloignement que les autres.
  – Je l'aime pourtant! se disait-elle.
  N'importe! elle n'était pas heureuse, ne l'avait jamais été. D'où
venait donc cette insuffisance de la vie, cette pourriture instantanée
des choses où elle s'appuyait?. . . Mais, s'il y avait quelque part un
être fort et beau, une nature valeureuse, pleine à la fois d'exaltation
et de raffinements, un cœur de poète sous une forme d'ange, lyre
aux cordes d'airain, sonnant vers le ciel des épithalames élégiaques,
pourquoi, par hasard, ne le trouverait-elle pas? Oh! quelle impossibilité! Rien, d'ailleurs, ne valait la peine d'une recherche; tout
mentait! Chaque sourire cachait un bâillement d'ennui, chaque joie une
malédiction, tout plaisir son dégoût, et les meilleurs baisers ne vous
laissaient sur la lèvre qu'une irréalisable envie d'une volupté plus haute.
  Un râle métallique se traîna dans les airs et quatre coups se firent
entendre à la cloche du couvent. Quatre heures! et il lui semblait qu'elle
était là, sur ce banc, depuis l'éternité. Mais un infini de passions peut
tenir dans une minute, comme une foule dans un petit espace.
  Emma vivait tout occupée des siennes, et ne s'inquiétait pas plus
de l'argent qu'une archiduchesse.
  Une fois pourtant, un homme d'allure chétive, rubicond et chauve,
entra chez elle, se déclarant envoyé par M.Vinçart, de Rouen.   (III,6)

(One day, when they had parted early and she was returning alone
along the boulevard, she saw the walls of her convent; she sat down
on a bench in the shade of the elms. How calm in those days! How
she longed for the ineffable sentiments of love which she had tried
to construct from the books she read!
  The first months of her marriage, her rides in the forest, the viscount waltzing with her, and Lagardy singing, everything passed again
before her eyes. . . And Léon suddenly appeared to her as distant
as the others.
  'Yet I love him', she told herself.
  No matter! She was not happy, never had been. Where did it come
from this inadequacy of life, this instantaneous putrefaction of
everything on which she leaned? . . . But if somewhere there were
a being strong and handsome, of valiant nature, both passionate and
refined, the heart of a poet in the form of an angel, a lyre with strings
of bronze raising elegiac epithalamia to the heavens, why, by chance,
should she not find him? Oh, how impossible! Besides, nothing was
worth the trouble of looking for; it was all lies! Every smile con-
cealed a yawn of boredom, every joy a curse, every pleasure its own
disgust, and the sweetest kisses left only on your lips the hopeless desire
for a higher delight.
  A metallic rattle trailed in the air and four strokes sounded from
the convent bell. Four o'clock! It seemed to her that she had been

sitting there on this bench from all eternity. But an infinity of passions can be contained in a minute, like a crowd in a small space.

Emma lived all absorbed in hers and worried no more about money than an archduchess.

There came a day, however, when a puny looking man with a red face and a bald head came to her house, saying he had been sent by Monsieur Vinçart of Rouen.)

The passage comes in the midst of the affair with Léon, at a time of lassitude and disillusionment, with Emma mixing lascivious abandonment (returning to him each time 'more avid and inflamed than before') and sickly sentimentalism (giving him a medallion of the Virgin to wear round his neck). Sitting under the wall of the convent of her school-days, Emma drifts into nostalgia, runs over her life, takes stock of her feelings.

The presentation of her thoughts is in *style indirect libre*, free indirect style, which begins at 'Quel calme dans ce temps-là!' and continues at various points in the following paragraphs. 'Tout mentait!' is Emma's perception now, after she has fallen once more into reverie and recited the novelistic fictions in which she would like to believe, 'Mais, s'il y avait quelque part un être fort et beau?'. The reflection is Emma's but the style modulates into irony, picking up the terms of her fantasy but going a little too far, a little beyond what her words and thoughts might be, which are thus in their essence exactly *and inordinately* expressed: 'un cœur de poète sous une forme d'ange, lyre aux cordes d'airain, sonnant vers le ciel des épithalames élégiaques'. Some day my prince will come. . . 'pourquoi, par hasard, ne le trouverait-elle pas?' 'Par hasard' is Emma's appeal to romantic chance, put down as hers and overturned: 'pourquoi ne le trouverait-elle pas?', we follow along in her fantasy but its flow is broken by the 'par hasard', inserted between commas almost as though set in quotation marks, underlining all this as Emma's and leaving us with the effect of an implacable copying, of platitude *pinned down*. In the one phrase, moreover, Flaubert condenses the deceit of Emma's fictions overall, picking up the recurrence of *hasard* as word and idea in her imaginings throughout the novel: 'She asked herself if it would not have been possible, by other combinations of chance [*par d'autres combinaisons du hasard*], to meet another man', I,7; 'Deep in her heart, however, she was waiting for something to happen. . . She had no idea what this chance would be [*quel serait ce hasard*], what wind would bring it to her, to what shore it would carry her', I,9; 'drawn to the man [Lagardy] through the illusion of the part he played, she tried to picture to herself the life he led, that splendid, extraordinary life of renown that might have been hers if chance had so wished it [*si le hasard l'avait voulu*], II,15; instead of which Emma is caught in the tedium of her provincial life which must, she deludedly and self-pityingly thinks, be an exception in the world, some 'unfortunate stroke of chance [*un hasard particulier*]' (I,9), and is left in the end to the violent inscription of chance on her body by the supreme representative of that life: 'Homais gave two or three great cuts at random [*au hasard*] that left white marks in that beautiful black hair', (III,9).

'Tout mentait!': she repeats her dreams but the repetition miscarries; she knows the falsehood of it all, everything lies. Where once she had excitedly cried 'I've a lover! a lover!', holding the reality to the magic words, she now tells herself she is in love without the words working any more, the 'yet' – *pourtant* – already marking the failure, their impossibility. 'N'importe!', no matter, so what? The words, her fictions, have no sense, no truth, are just a cheat. What is real is the putrefaction of things, the truth of the blind man's decomposing flesh, his voice, too, trailing in the air, like the convent bell: 'It went to the very depths of her soul like a whirlwind in an abyss, and swept her away into the expanse of a boundless melancholy' (III,5). The blind man enters later in the novel but his cry, metallic and dragging, is strangely there already, in echo, when Emma yields to Rodolphe in the forest: 'Then, far away, beyond the wood, on the other hills, she heard a vague, prolonged cry, a voice which trailed along, and she silently listened to it, mingling like music with the last vibrations of her nerves in passion' (II,9). As the novel draws her story to its close, cry and echoes intensify, grating on the settled order of the Homais world, as Emma grates too, her very body finally joining with the blind man's to represent the atrocious farce of existence: so we have the blind man's 'weak and whining voice', growing sharper as he hangs on to the coach that brings Emma back from Rouen (III,5); the metallic rattle of the convent bell in the present passage; the 'deafening metallic vibration' of the cart that goes violently by after the masked ball (III,6); the 'sharp cry' Emma utters as the poison grips her, at one with the blind man in her contorted, dying body (III,8); the blind man's voice again, in raucous song, that, at the moment of Emma's death rattle, interrupts Charles's sobs and Bournisien's Latin ('Emma sat up, like a galvanised corpse', *ibid*).

'D'où venait donc cette insuffisance de la vie, cette pourriture instantanée des choses où elle s'appuyait?' The question is Emma's and more than Emma's; it represents what she has come to feel but stands too as a more general representation, recognises a truth wider than her particular case. Putrefaction, decay, rottenness, are the book's continual facts, its powerful images: Hippolyte's gangrenous leg ('A livid tumescence spread over the whole leg, with pustules here and there from which a black liquid oozed', II,11), the blind man's rotting face ('The flesh was tearing into red strips, and from them flowed a liquid which congealed in green scabs down to his nose', III,5), and then finally Emma's corpse ('It was necessary to raise her head a little, and as they did so a stream of black liquid came from her mouth, as though she were vomiting', III,9). 'D'où venait donc. . .': the question follows Emma's thinking and at the same time, in its language, its emphasis, implies a narration that concurs in this view of things. Before putrefaction — but putrefaction is always already the case — comes merely life, 'a hope and a deception', as the young Flaubert defines it (*SNPI*, 35); which is what Emma's story plays out, summarised in the present passage in the syntax of her developing reflection: 'Je l'aime pourtant. . . N'importe! elle n'était pas heureuse. . . Mais, s'il y avait quelque part. . . Oh! quelle impossibilité! Rien, d'ailleurs. . . tout mentait!' The passage gives us a position as readers of Emma's story, its events ('Une fois, pourtant'), offers the distance of commentary ('Emma. . . ne s'inquiétait pas plus de l'argent qu'une archiduchesse'), exposes her dreams ('Mais, s'il y avait quelque part'), but modulates as well into an involvement of narrating voice and reader, we sharing with her what becomes an overall vision: 'tout mentait! Chaque sourire cachait un bâillement d'ennui, chaque joie une malédiction, tout plaisir son dégoût, et les meilleurs baisers ne vous laissaient sur la lèvre qu'une irréalisable envie d'une volupté plus haute.' Emma represents the ineluctable cycle of desire and disillusion, and the representation includes book and reader; the *vous* is both Emma's self-address in indirect free speech and the book's address to the reader, caught up in that *vous*, the complicity that indirect free speech can effect: Emma and Flaubert and we as readers are together in the voice here, bound to this question and its vision, life as a hope and a deception – everything lies.

Impersonality is a goal, the very condition of art and its disengagement from the lies, but Flaubert's novel has a voice nevertheless, a narrational point of view which is manifest at moments, in different ways. One way is quite simply as a source of direct knowledge: knowledge of the narrative and its agents, setting out the story and describing the behaviour and thoughts of the characters (for example, what Charles does and thinks during Emma's post-Rodolphe collapse, II,14); knowledge of the social–cultural context, what this world is like (for example, peacocks are 'the luxury of Cauchois farmyards', I,2); knowledge of the ways of the world, offering a kind of social–cultural psychology (for example, noting Léon's new Parisian confidence in the face of 'this insignificant doctor's wife': 'Self-assurance depends on environment. One does not speak the same language in a drawing-room as in an attic; and the wealthy woman seems to have all her bank-notes about her to protect her virtue, like so much armour-plate in the lining of her corset', III,1). Flaubert is far from the model of the Balzac novel, but close too, able to demonstrate a similar confidence of social understanding and worldly insight (as in the example just quoted on 'self-assurance').

One instance of a narrating voice, presented as such, has often troubled readers: the *nous* that appears with the first word of the novel only to disappear a few pages later: 'We were in class', 'Nous étions à l'Etude' (I,1). Satre called it 'a mistake', and this has been a not uncommon response, the narrating *nous* seen as out of place in a novel seeking the effect of impersonality, and with this out-of-placeness seemingly acknowledged by its sudden abandonment (the drafts here move between the *nous* and a *je*, a particular 'I'-witness from within the collective 'we'-memory). The *nous*, moreover, has a certain awkwardness of status, proposed as if by someone able to recall Charles's school-days yet simultaneously unable to remember him at all: 'It would be impossible now for any of us to remember anything about him' (*ibid*); at which point the *nous* vanishes from the book, but then only after a great deal *has* been remembered about Charles's behaviour at school and his family background.

At the time of the novel's publication, there was doubtless little problem (contemporary readers had no access to the letters, no developed expectations of impersonality). Flaubert adopts a conventional narrative strategy, beginning with a narrator–companion of the hero who introduces him in an unproblematic mix of personally authenticated narration and (what is in effect) omniscient report which the former simply contains (the description of Charles's life prior to his going to school is a third-person account placed within the *nous*-narration). Balzac, for example, uses this strategy in *Louis Lambert* (1832), written through a narrator who was a school friend of the hero and who comes and goes as *je* and *nous* as he recounts Louis's career from his school-days onwards. It remains, however, that Charles is not the central figure of Flaubert's novel and that the *nous*-narrator is short-lived, a sign of impotence and erasure, it being impossible now to remember anything of him − where 'him' might just as well refer to the narrator as to Charles, the narrator who is promptly forgotten the moment he declares his own forgetting.

The *nous* and its disappearance involve more than convention, just as they are more significant than any dismissal as some 'mistake' would allow. There is a trace of Flaubert in this *nous* memory of the Collège de Rouen, a memory that is longer in the drafts and that the *je* there underlines, personalises a little more. Flaubert, indeed, had already written this same scene of the schoolboy mocked by his classmates in the autobiographical *Mémoires d'un fou*. Except that there the narrator is the boy himself, and the boy is not Charles and stupid but Flaubert and mad, raging at the stupidity around him: 'The imbeciles! Them, laughing at me!' (*OC* I, 232). The shift from the *je* of *Mémoires* to the imbecile 'Charbovari', from the personal memory − or the creation of a personal memory − to the depersonalisation of the memory, held at the distance of Charles and forgotten, impossible *now*, captures the movement to impersonality involved in the writing of *Madame Bovary*. *Mémoires d'un fou* is also impossible now, there can be no memory of those memoir–memories: what is left, what could be left of Flaubert the collegian, the romantic, of the school-days group of young hotbloods (remember that, in fact, the Collège de Rouen was where Flaubert found his literary beginnings, had a *pléiade* of convivial friends), of all the aspiration of adolescence? Nothing. Nothing but this trace nevertheless, the appearance–disappearance of memory at the start of this new experimental work, the break into Art; nothing also, then, but the dissemination of the author − nowhere visible, everywhere present − that the desired impersonality is about.

The *nous* and its disappearance, that is, have their significance in the novel. The *nous* is centred on Charles and Charles *will* be forgotten, or at least displaced from the centre: this is not his novel but Emma's, and we modulate from the one to the other, from him to her as central perspective, the figure in whom Flaubert's memory, his desire, will be at stake − she, after all, will be the isolated subject, the romantic, the mad one. The present time of the opening narration − 'Il serait maintenant impossible' − returns at the end of the novel, stressed in the very last words: 'Il vient de recevoir la croix d'honneur', 'He has just been given the Legion of Honour' (III,11). Emma's story is past, over at the start, enclosed between Charles and Homais, held within the world of men, the contemporary stupidity; something the narration records in its little scenario of the shift from *nous* and author–memory to the novel's story of Emma, and from that to the present *il* of Homais, the bourgeois, the other.

The abandonment of the declared *nous*-narrator is not, however, the disappearance of any narrating voice. In addition to the voicings of knowledge mentioned earlier, there is the introduction of direct commentary on characters and events: 'Thus there stood, before those beaming bourgeois, half a century of servitude' (on Catherine Leroux, II,8); 'A fine voice, colossal aplomb, more temperament than intelligence and more grandiloquence than lyricism, all lending the finishing touches to this admirable charlatan-type, in which there was something of both the hairdresser and the bullfighter' (on Lagardy, II,15); 'with that coward's courage that nothing can stop' (on Léon, III,1). Such commentary, as these examples show, is far from gentle; it serves above all to state weakness, insincerity, self-delusion, and most especially in relation to Emma: 'So she set out for La Huchette, without realising that she was hastening to expose herself to what a little while before had so angered her, nor conscious in the least of this prostitution' (III,7); 'She was corrupting him from beyond the grave' (III,9).

In counterpart to which there is also an occasional direct evasion of narrational omniscience: ' "No doubt", replied the doctor indifferently either because, sharing the same ideas, he wished to offend no one or because he had no ideas' (II,14); 'she pretended to believe, or perhaps believed, in the pretext he gave for their break' (III,8). More interestingly, from the drafts to the final version, Flaubert made cuts and revisions which leave the causality of the novel, the sense of its direction, unsure. This can involve quite simple details of explanation: on the day of the agricultural show, Emma suddenly appears in the street on Rodolphe's arm, where a draft told how 'He had called at her house just before the show' (*NV*, 348–9); Rodolphe draws up three stools for himself and Emma in the town hall and a draft provided the reason for the 'three', 'so that she could sit down and put her feet up' (*NV*, 353). The removal of such details adds to the feeling of a world impersonally presented, not anchored in explanation, producing a hesitation in reading: Homais, in his inimitable welcoming speech on Yonville's climate, erroneously gives 54 degrees

Fahrenheit as equivalent to 24 degrees Réaumur, which is somewhat motivated in a draft by the general comment that he 'is a little careless as to exactitude' (*NV*, 60); the elimination of this comment leaves the reading caught between error on Flaubert's part and irony against Homais, or, if the error goes unrecognised, irony against the reader (itself then unrecognised, other than from above, 'the superior farce'). As well as details of this kind, the work from drafts to final version involved the suppression of a host of comments, and comparisons serving as comments, particularly those relating to the presentation of Emma and the emphasis on her debauchery. For example, the description of her times with Léon in their hotel room had a scene in which he cut his finger and she sucked his blood 'like a coiled serpent silently feasting' (*NV*, 538).

Emma lies, but everything lies: the narrating voice enters to state a distance from her, to condemn (this increasingly towards the end of the novel, as though drawing away from her to a close), but Flaubert also cuts such statements, reduces their number (the prosecution at the trial cannot see any). The comments that are left, moreover, are problematic. To talk of Emma's 'prostitution' may be right but the word can be used just as well of Homais: 'he sold himself, he prostituted himself' (III,11). In a world of prostitution, the word applied to Emma has no particular significance, is from the overall critique of this whole world which Emma herself is also making, for which she is the novel's figure. Furthermore, a narrating voice mouthing 'prostitution' risks finding itself at one with the voices of Mesdames Bovary mother, Tuvache *et al.*, risks falling in with some given discourse and repeating its received ideas. Truth is in impersonality; or silence, as occasionally for the novel in Justin's silences or Charles's failures to find words or Emma's moments of stillness: 'She abandoned herself to him. . . Silence was everywhere; something sweet seemed to come forth from the trees; she felt her heart begin to beat again, and the blood flowing in her flesh like a river of milk' (II,9). There is no simple assertion of silence as value − Justin is also an infatuated adolescent, Charles is mediocre and empty, the silence in the wood is broken by the discordant cry in the

distance — but, in the midst of the platitudes, there is
something to be grasped in what is said in the absence of words,
or under words, or even, nevertheless, in words. Condemned
to trivial phrases, commonplace images, Emma's feelings are
also real, intense; her puerile sentimentalisms of language have
something substantial to express:

> [Rodolphe] had heard these things said so many times that they
> had nothing original for him. Emma was like all mistresses; and the
> charm of novelty, gradually falling away like a garment, laid bare
> the eternal monotony of passion, whose forms and language are always
> the same. This man of experience was unable to perceive the difference
> of feelings under the equivalence of expressions. Because wanton or
> mercenary lips had murmured similar phrases, he only faintly be-
> lieved in the candour of Emma's; one had to make allowances, he
> thought, exaggerated declarations masking mediocre affection; as
> though the fullness of the soul did not sometimes overflow in the most
> empty metaphors, since no one ever can give the exact measure of
> their needs, their thoughts or their sorrows, and human language is
> like a cracked cauldron on which we beat out tunes to make a bear
> dance when we would move the stars to pity.   (II,12)

The passage shifts from Emma to everyone, to the statement
that we can none of us give any exact expression to our needs
or thoughts or sorrows, to the poignant image of the cracked
cauldron of human language. If we take statement and image
seriously, as we must, then we are brought back to the double
reality of Flaubert's novel, irony *and lyricism*. Impersonality
gives not just the former, the unnerving flatness of the copy,
but also the latter, the disturbing possibility at any moment,
in exactly those copied words, of the overflowing of something
else, some reality of feeling that can have no expression but
in the misheard, misread monotony of the usual stereotyped
forms. Flaubert is ironist and lyricist, and Emma, commonplace and intense, is the figure — the truth — of those
modes together.

The art of the novel

'How many devices it takes to be true!'   (6 April 1853, C)

A key device in the achievement of Flaubert's impersonality is *style indirect libre*. This can be found in writing before Flaubert – notably in English in the works of Jane Austen – and goes along with the general development of a psychologically intimate novel, involving the presentation of the inner life of its characters. Flaubert in *Madame Bovary*, however, is decisively innovative in the extensive use he makes of this style to place the reader within the very terms of such interiority and in his simultaneous realisation of it as a mode of ironic hesitation, citing the characters in their discourse, their trains of thought, in such a way as to leave the reader hesitating between character and commentary, not knowing whether to take what is said at face value with the character in question, or to read it at some distance of reflection on him or her. Flaubert, it should be noted, did not himself have the term *style indirect libre* and says little in the correspondence that bears immediately on it; what was at stake for him, that is, was not so much a particular procedure as an overall vision that determined its elaboration and use: free indirect style followed from the Flaubertian imperative of impersonality.

Consider this passage from the account of Emma in the attic room reading Rodolphe's farewell letter:

> Elle jetait les yeux tout autour d'elle avec l'envie que la terre croulât. Pourquoi n'en pas finir? Qui la retenait donc? Elle était libre. Et elle s'avança, elle regarda les pavés en se disant:
> – Allons! allons!   (II,13)

> She stared about her wishing that the earth might give way. Why not have done with it all? Who was to stop her? She was free. She moved forward and looked down at the paving-stones, saying to herself, 'Go on! Go on!')

The first sentence narrates Emma's action and state of mind in the third person of narrative report; what we know of her thoughts is given indirectly, is recounted: 'Elle jetait les yeux tout autour d'elle avec l'envie que la terre croulât.' The last sentence returns to third-person narration, 'elle s'avança', but closes with a direct presentation of her inner words, 'Allons! allons!' In between, there is something else: 'Pourquoi n'en pas finir? Qui la retenait donc? Elle était libre.' These are Emma's very questions and thoughts, her very formulations to herself, yet given indirectly: 'Qui la retenait donc?' is what she thinks but transposed from what would have been her direct 'Qui me retient?' The direct personal has been absorbed into a third-person narration which at the same time is not simply that of an indirect account, as in 'Elle se demandait qui la retenait.' The sentence 'Elle était libre' equally participates in this style, comes from what she inwardly tells herself: 'Je suis libre', another illusion and fiction and lie, since she is not, she is Madame Bovary; and anyway freedom and fate are complexly envisaged in the book in a way that allows no such assertion an unproblematic value; and anyway again, the assertion comes with a touch of the novels and romances Emma reads, is a rhetorical gesture from their world; but then, on top of all that, the ever-circling irony, Emma *is* in a novel, and she *does* kill herself, and there is an anticipation here of the book to come and its overall vision: why not indeed have done with it all?

'Elle était libre': the sentence is read as Emma's, but nothing indicates that she possesses that sentence, that it is hers. Suppose it were that of the narration, a statement from a narrating voice declaring her to be free. The point would then be not so much Emma's illusion, the irony to be derived from that, but rather the double-edged strategy of a narrating voice ironically pointing to the limits of her freedom by this contrary assertion that simultaneously has its own ironic truth: she *is* free to kill herself (though, again, that freedom is determined, 'the fault of fate'; a view that in turn falls under multiple ironies). Relatively simple in this example, one of the major possibilities of this style of presentation is just such an oscillation: how can it be stopped, tied down to this or that position, this or that reading, without it slipping away, twisting round again, flipping over into other potential readings? As used by Flaubert, it becomes the very mode of impersonality as undecidable, beyond conclusions; orders of language, versions of sense, can be set down with no commitment, so many quotations which the writer neither accepts nor evidently condemns (which would be merely to take up another conclusive position), remaining in suspense in the work.

Style indirect libre thus involves the use of the actual mode of expression of a character but embedded in the narrative telling, with the grammatical forms assimilated to those of reported speech – the character's thought or speech is partly, but only partly, re-phrased to fit the past tense of the narration. 'She said: "No, I can't just now" ' is an example of speech represented directly, her exact words. 'She said that she couldn't just then' is one of indirect representation, we are told what she said in a third-person narration. 'She looked away. No, she couldn't just then. Perhaps some other time. She turned over the pages of her diary' gives us speech in free indirect style; what she said is not represented directly, it is embedded in the narrative telling, at the same time that there is an incorporation of her actual words, grammatically transposed where necessary so as to permit the embedding (from first person to third, from present to past: 'No, *I can't* just *now*'/'No, *she couldn't* just *then*'; note that 'Perhaps some other time' requires no transpositions). 'Free' (*style indirect* libre) refers to the way in which this form of reporting speech is free from the markers, the constraints, of indirect reported speech – 'she said that', and so on – and can allow this kind of incorporation of direct elements, close up to the character in her or his own terms.

Some simple examples will show the quite general use of free indirect style in *Madame Bovary*:

Mais, à tout cela, M. Bovary, peu soucieux des lettres, disait que ce *n'était pas la peine*! Auraient-ils jamais de quoi l'entretenir dans les écoles du gouvernment, lui acheter une charge ou un fonds de commerce? D'ailleurs, *avec du toupet, un homme réussit toujours dans le monde*. Madame Bovary se mordait les lèvres, et l'enfant vagabondait dans le village.   (I,1)

(To all of which, Monsieur Bovary, caring little for education, said that it *wasn't worth the trouble*! How would they ever be able to keep the boy at a government school, to buy him a post or set him up in business? Besides, *with a bit of nerve a man can always get on in the world*. Madame Bovary bit her lip and the boy knocked about the village.)

Dès qu'ils furent seuls, M. Lheureux se mit, en termes assez nets, à féliciter Emma sur la succession, puis à causer de choses indifférentes, des espaliers, de la récolte et de sa santé à lui, qui allait toujours *couci-couci, entre le zist et le zest*. En effet, il se donnait un mal de cinq cents diables, bien qu'il ne fît pas, malgré les propos du monde, de quoi avoir seulement du beurre sur son pain. (III,2)

(As soon as they were alone, Monsieur Lheureux began to congratulate Emma in pretty plain terms on the inheritance. Then he went on to neutral topics, the fruit trees, the harvest, his own health which was always *up and down, only so-so*. Indeed, he had to work like the very devil and, whatever people might say, still didn't make enough to put butter on his bread.)

Il ne plaisantait pas; mais, la vanité l'emportant sur toute prudence, Léon, malgré lui, se récria. 'D'ailleurs, il n'aimait que les femmes brunes. (III,6)

(He [Homais] was perfectly serious, but Léon, vanity overcoming all prudence, protested in spite of himself. Anyway, he only liked dark women.)

The simplicity of these examples comes from the relative monotony of the characters involved, whose speech and thoughts are easily identifiable, readily allowing the reader to assume the distance from them of the novel's narration, with the risk of confusion of voice and position therefore limited. Lheureux's cunningly obsequious commercial patter can instantly be heard, as too can Bovary father's old soldier's no-nonsense scorn for his wife's wish to educate Charles; and we are brought up flat against the very movement of Léon's bathetic ordinariness, the snobbish vanity that compels him to object when Homais teases him with having courted Emma's maid: 'D'ailleurs, il n'aimait que les femmes brunes', where the 'D'ailleurs' modulates us into free indirect style, into Léon's spoken protest ('D'ailleurs, je n'aime que les femmes brunes'). In two of these examples, moreover, Flaubert has placed certain words or phrases in italics, underlining the presence of the character's own language, the fact of the embedding. Twice the italics come at the point at which indirect speech will shift into free indirect style: 'disait que ce *n'était pas la peine*! Auraient-ils jamais. . .'; or at which the shift is being

made: 'se mit. . . à causer. . . de sa santé à lui, qui allait toujours *couci-couci, entre le zist et le zest*. En effet. . .' (the shift
comes with 'qui allait toujours', then confirmed in the italics);
while the third use of italics emphasises a characteristic turn
of phrase within the run of a passage in free indirect style, in
this case coming to the conclusion of father Bovary's 'reason-
ing' as he throws in a favourite maxim: '*avec du toupet, un
homme réussit toujours dans le monde*' (*toupet* is familiar,
popular, like Lheureux's *couci-couci*, and indicates straight-
away a voice that is not that of the narration, is immediately,
as it were, in italics).

Italics here nail the commonplace, setting it off from the
language of the narration. They identify the *on dit* of language,
its 'what-is-said': Emma in her convent had received 'comme
on dit, *une belle éducation*' (I,2; 'what is called *a good education*'); Charles's parents fall out with his first wife and leave
his house, 'Mais *le coup était porté*. Huit jours après. . . elle
fut prise d'un crachement de sang' (*ibid.*, 'But *the blow had
struck home*. A week later. . . she began to spit blood'). The
second example dispenses with the *comme on dit* which is
anyway redundant, contained in the italics which indicate an
habitual, empty phrase. It is no surprise that Homais, supreme
figure of the commonplace, *speaks* in italics, quotes himself
quoting: 'Je vous trouve jolie comme un Amour! Vous allez
faire florès à Rouen' (II,14; 'You're as pretty as a picture.
You'll be a *big hit* in Rouen'). Yet where should the italics begin
and end? 'Jolie comme un Amour' is as italicisable as '*faire
florès*'; as indeed is everything else, since language in its essence
is the locus of the *comme on dit*, and Flaubert too is caught
in this *on*, held like everyone else to the given language and
all its compulsions of meaning. The whole book should be in
italics, which is the very project of the *Dictionnaire des idées
recues*, but also of *Madame Bovary* in its impersonality of free
indirect style, with Flaubert not owning to any of the words
and phrases he thereby *quotes*, puts into silent italics, avoiding
any loud positions.

Flaubert's development of free indirect style is thus towards
a use of its possibilities of simultaneous closeness to and separation from the characters's thought and expression that allows

for much more complex effects than the more *evident* examples
so far discussed:

> Emma se répétait:
> — Pourquoi, mon Dieu! me suis-je mariée?
>
> Elle se demandait s'il n'y aurait pas eu moyen, par d'autres
> combinaisons du hasard, de rencontrer un autre homme; et elle
> cherchait à imaginer quels eussent été ces événements non survenus,
> cette vie différente, ce mari qu'elle ne connaissait pas. Tous, en effet,
> ne ressemblaient pas à celui-là. Il aurait pu être beau, spirituel, distingué,
> attirant, tels qu'ils étaient sans doute, ceux qu'avaient épousés ses
> anciennes camarades du couvent. Que faisaient-elles maintenant? A la
> ville, avec le bruit des rues, le bourdonnement des théâtres et les clartés
> du bal, elles avaient des existences où le cœur se dilate, où les sens
> s'épanouissent. Mais elle, sa vie était froide comme un grenier dont la
> lucarne est au nord, et l'ennui, araignée silencieuse, filait sa toile dans
> l'ombre à tous les coins de son cœur. Elle se rappelait les jours de distribu-
> tion de prix, où elle montait sur l'estrade pour aller chercher ses petites
> couronnes. Avec ses cheveux en tresse, sa robe blanche et ses souliers de
> prunelle découverts, elle avait une façon gentille, et les messieurs, quand
> elle regagnait sa place, se penchaient pour lui faire des compliments; la
> cour était pleine de calèches, on lui disait adieu par les portières, le maître
> de musique passait en saluant, avec sa boîte à violon. Comme c'était loin,
> tout cela! comme c'était loin!
>
> Elle appelait Djali, la prenait entre ses genoux, passait ses doigts
> sur sa longue tête fine et lui disait:
> — Allons, baisez maîtresse, vous qui n'avez pas de chagrins. (I,7)

(Emma repeated to herself, 'Why, in God's name, did I get
married?'

She wondered if by some other workings of chance it would not
have been possible for her to meet some other man; and she tried to
imagine what those unrealised events, that different life, that unknown
husband would have been. For all husbands were not like hers. He
might have been handsome, witty, distinguished, attractive, as no
doubt were the men her old friends from the convent had married.
What were they doing now? In town, with the bustle of the streets,
the hum of the theatres and the bright lights of the ballroom, they
were living lives where the heart swells and the senses bloom. As for
her, her life was as cold as an attic with its window facing north, and
the silent spider boredom wove its web in the shadows in every cor-
ner of her heart. She remembered prize-giving days, going up on the
platform to receive her little crowns. With her plaited hair, her white
frock and her open prunella shoes, she had a pretty way and the
gentlemen in the audience would lean over to congratulate her as she
went back to her seat; the courtyard was full of carriages, people said

goodbye to her from their windows, the music-master bowed as he passed with his violin case. How far away that all was! How far away!

She called Djali, took the dog between her knees and stroked its long, delicate head, saying 'Come, kiss mistress, you who have no sorrows.')

Emma in Tostes, newly married, rehearses her disillusion and turns to her imagination of what might have been. Her process of reflection is reported indirectly, 'Elle se demandait. . . elle cherchait à imaginer', with a shift into the closeness of free indirect style: 'Tous, en effet, ne ressemblait pas à celui-là. . . Il aurait pu être beau. . . Que faisaient-elles maintenant?. . . Mais elle, sa vie était froide. . . Comme c'était loin, tout cela! comme c'était loin!' Within this rendering of Emma's inner speech, there are evident moments at which the writing outruns her own formulations; the images − 'sa vie était froide comme un grenier dont la lucarne est au nord', 'l'ennui, araignée silencieuse, filait sa toile dans l'ombre' − are not Emma's, but those of the narration describing her, capturing the nature of the coldness and boredom she feels. Yet where there is a ready dissociation from her version of the husband she might have had, from her self-pitying conviction − 'sans doute' − that all her schoolfriends have the life she lacks, these images give us a certain complicity of the narration with Emma's reflection, an acceptance of her point of view. Emma feels the coldness of her life, the narration supports her with an image; Emma feels lassitude, the narration takes over the knowledge of that *ennui*, puts it on the page for the reader through the elaboration of the image of the spider's silent weaving of its web. Emma's romance of what might have been and her nostalgic reworking of herself as centre of attention on prize-giving days with her nice white dress and winning manner with the gentlemen (a seduction scenario that will have its echoes in her subsequent career) are hers alone, at the distance the writing and the reader have from her; the coldness, the lassitude, the emptiness of the world in which she finds herself, however, are equally a reality for writing and reader, at one with Emma on this. At the close of the passage the narration sets Emma apart again in externally seen gesture and directly reported speech as she calls her dog and strikes a melancholy pose: 'vous qui n'avez pas de chagrins'. This comes back on, but without cancelling out, the previous closeness, which was there too in the immediately preceding 'Comme c'était loin, tout cela! comme c'était loin!' The latter is itself, moreover, an echo at once of a previous free indirect style presentation of her father, he also remembering Emma's childhood – 'Comme c'était vieux, tout cela!' (I,4) – and of the opening of the novel, remembering Charles's schooldays as a past beyond remembrance: everything is over, past, for Emma and for the narration, the two as one in the knowledge of the absence of any present – any present beyond *ennui*, the actuality of its image, the silent spider.

Style indirect libre affords the possibility, as it were, of a kind of critical fusion; the writer and the reader become Emma, are taken up in her reverie, her imaginings, but with an edge of distance that can at any moment be more or less apparent and so more or less equivocal, exploited for a whole range of effects. Between the separated closeness of direct first-person speech and thought, giving the characters in their own clearly identified terms, set off as such, and the assured distance of third-person indirect report, giving the characters within an overall framework of external depiction, recounted by a narrating voice, free indirect style can offer a paradoxical uncertainty of closeness and distance, of hesitation over the one or the other. This is fundamental for Flaubert's 'identification' with his heroine as expressing his intimate themes of desire and disillusion, and his simultaneous disengagement as artist from any self-assured personal standpoint, from implication in the social mediocrity that Emma's story serves to reveal: the writer in free indirect style moves into discourses without assuming any one as his – Flaubert's – identity, but without the assumption either of some narrative metalanguage, the authorised position of a third-person reporter and commentator (such a reporter–commentator nevertheless, as we have seen, has a partial existence: managing the knowledge of the novel's world, but also intervening at points to state its mediocrity, as though Flaubert is unable fully to contain the loathing that defines the very necessity for impersonality, for

staying free from any commitment within the mediocre world).
Discourses are put into play and the reader hesitates as to how
to take what is said, how to conclude a reading — there is an
irony of undecidability.

Here is Homais, who has named one of his daughters Athalie
in homage to Racine's play, 'the most immortal masterpiece
of the French stage':

Car ses convictions philosophiques n'empêchaient pas ses admirations
artistiques, le penseur chez lui n'étouffait point l'homme sensible; il
savait établir des différences, faire la part de l'imagination et celle
du fanatisme. De cette tragédie, par exemple, il blâmait les idées, mais
il admirait le style; il maudissait la conception, mais il applaudissait
à tous les détails, et s'exaspérait contre les personnages, en s'en-
thousiasmant de leurs discours. Lorsqu'il lisait les grands morceaux,
il était transporté; mais, quand il songeait que les calotins en tiraient
avantage pour leur boutique, il était désolé, et dans cette confusion
de sentiments où il s'embarrassait, il aurait voulu tout à la fois pouvoir
couronner Racine de ses deux mains et discuter avec lui pendant un
bon quart d'heure.   (II,3)

(For his philosophical convictions did not prevent his artistic
appreciation; in him the thinker in no way stifled the man of feeling;
he could make distinctions, draw the line between imagination and
fanaticism. In this tragedy of *Athalie*, for example, he censured the
ideas but admired the style; he inveighed against the conception but
applauded the execution, was exasperated at the characters while
enthusiastic for their speeches. When he read the great passages, he
was carried away; but when he remembered that the holy lot were
turning them to the advantage of their trade, he was mortified and,
in this confusion of feelings, he would have liked simultaneously to
crown Racine with his own two hands and to take him to task for
a good quarter of an hour.)

The final sentence gives us a straightforward narrational report
(but with the report including something of Homais's own
language, 'quand il songeait que *les calotins en tiraient avantage
pour leur boutique*'), closing with what comes as the epitomisa-
tion of the self-conceit of the man — Homais who would like
to put Racine right. Similarly, the passage as a whole gives us
a character-sketch of Homais through the straightforward
description of his attitude to the arts, his response to Racine.
But who is speaking in the initial development, 'Car ses con-

victions philosophiques. . .'? This is Homais's own vision, the smug discourse of his vainglory ('chez moi, voyez-vous, le penseur n'étouffe nullement l'homme sensible'); but at the same time it is the voice of the narration, setting Homais up in all his stupidity, feigning a sympathetically balanced account that is read as ferociously ironical: 'le penseur chez lui n'étouffait point l'homme sensible'. The hesitation here around *style indirect libre* − Homais's voice or a narrator's − is in a way unimportant: either or both together come out as the same ridicule, though the hesitation unsettles any hold on a declared position of narrating voice, runs into the effect of impersonality. The initial development might still, however, be straight narration, the voice of a steady, true description informing us that in Homais the thinker does indeed not smother the man of feeling. The reading, in other words, could slide into taking the development at face value, neither free indirect style nor ironic narration; after all, *Homais* would read it precisely this way, as flatly correct, a perfectly valid account, which, ironically too, it is ('I who find [Homais's views] highly grotesque will no doubt be properly had, since for the bourgeois it's all very reasonable', 26 April 1853, C).

The example, in fact, has its limits. The context and movement of the passage, everything we know of Homais, the myriad examples of his colossal aplomb, lead us away from reading as he would and taking it as written out of an admiration in which we are being invited to acquiesce: the passage can be counted on to 'self-destruct', to ironise itself. But even then not entirely counted on, there is still some room for doubt, and we have to remember again Flaubert's idea of a book in which readers would be unable to decide whether or not they were being fooled, would never be clear as to how they should read (it is the reader finally who is to be properly had, left caught irresolvably between the grotesque and the reasonable).

Here is Emma at home in front of the mirror after she has given herself to Rodolphe in the wood:

Elle se répétait: 'J'ai un amant! un amant!' se délectant à cette idée comme à celle d'une autre puberté qui lui serait survenue. Elle allait donc posséder enfin ces joies de l'amour, cette fièvre du bonheur dont elle avait désespéré. Elle entrait dans quelque chose de merveilleux où tout serait passion, extase, délire; une immensité bleuâtre l'entourait, les sommets du sentiment étincelaient sous sa pensée, et l'existence ordinaire n'apparaissait qu'au loin, tout en bas, dans l'ombre, entre les intervalles de ces hauteurs.   (II,9)

(She repeated to herself 'I've a lover, a lover!', delighting in the idea as if in some second puberty. So at last she was to know those joys of love, that fever of happiness of which she had despaired. She was entering upon something marvellous where it would all be passion, ecstasy, delirium; a blue-tinged immensity lay around her, the high peaks of feeling sparkled beneath her mind, and ordinary life appeared only in the far distance, way below, in the shadows, in the gaps between those heights.)

The passage offers Emma's vision of her happiness to come, the idea − based on her novels and their 'lyrical legion' of adulterous heroines − of what it is to have 'a lover!', of what the liaison with Rodolphe will be. We as readers know that this is illusion, have seen who Rodolphe really is (his cynical seduction), who Emma is (the fantasies she indulges), what their reality is (the Yonville world of Homais, Binet, Bovary *et al.*): the writing takes us identifiably into Emma's thoughts and the shift into *style indirect libre* at 'Elle allait donc posséder. . .' poses no problem; this is Emma's reverie, we know where we are, we follow her illusion at a distance even as we are held close to it. Yet there is also some truth: she *will* know that fever of happiness. And perhaps there may be a question after all as regards identifying who is speaking. The passage was read at the trial, with the prosecutor moving from a reading of the voice as Emma's, 'she glorifies adultery', to a reading of it as that of the narration, of the book itself, 'this glorification of adultery'. To assign the passage to Emma is both easy and not quite so easy, the origin even here is open to uncertainty; free indirect style does not give some declared determination of reading (of the kind that would be found had Flaubert written 'elle se disait qu'elle allait posséder enfin'). Report − here's what Emma thought − spirals into assertion − yes, at last she was going to have those joys of love − and back and round again: the reading could go wrong. Except, again, that it would not be *just* wrong: Emma's illusion is also real, has its truth of desire, against the mediocrity of her world; and Flaubert, his writing of this novel, is as close to as he is distant from Emma; which is exactly the undecidability, the impersonality of position that *style indirect libre* can achieve. The story is to tell itself, and the reader is to derive unity from the work in its totality, not from any controlling authorial voice within it. 'It is a delicious thing to write, no longer to be *oneself* but to circulate in the whole creation of which one speaks' (23 December 1853, C). Free indirect style furnishes the particular realisation in *Madame Bovary* of just such a circulation: the author projects himself into his characters, but they are held within an overall narration of which this style is the unsettling mode. Its focalisation, *with* the characters, *in* their speech and thought, produces an impersonality whose point, through this style of effacement, is the possibility of the author's presence nowhere graspable as such, with any position of a narrator constantly slipping away in the turns of reading it brings.

While *style indirect libre* is fundamental, there are other procedures that concur with it in the art of Flaubert's novel and the particular realisation of impersonality. Thus discourses are juxtaposed, so as to cancel each other out in an irony that need take no side but only bear witness to their mutual nullification. The obvious example of this ironic montage is the famous account of the agricultural show which intercuts the speech made by the Prefect's representative with Rodolphe's seduction of Emma; the rhetoric of work, religion and civilisation with that of fate, love and passion: 'Rodolphe was talking dreams, forebodings, magnetism with Madame Bovary. Going back to the cradle of society, the orator painted those fierce times when men lived on acorns in the heart of woods' (II,8). Another clear example is the movement back and forth between Homais's fatuous disquisition on the climate and society of Yonville and Emma's conversation with Léon on the poetry of seas and setting suns (II,2). But the novel throughout is involved in such effects, more often on a smaller scale, insidious rather than manifest: little bits of language to set one another off, side by side in mutual annulment, so many counter-reacting *idées reçues*.

The corollary of this montage is the absence of dialogue. No one talks to anyone else, just as no one listens: conversation is an exchange of monologues and everyone *is* their monologue, the particular frame of language they happen to be in; when Homais meets Madame Le François, she counters his set of ready phrases with hers, 'one must move with the times' with 'as long as the *Lion d'Or* exists, people will come' (II,1). It makes no difference if the same set is shared: Emma and Léon merely monologue with each other from within their common idiom, assenting to its repetition − 'How true! How true!' − and rehearsing its variations − 'but now I love stories that rush along in one breath, that frighten you' (II,2). To listen is to be trapped in the language one wants to hear, in which the other is imagined; so Emma listens to Rodolphe, incapable of conceiving him outside of the novelistic discourse she expects and that he does, indeed, recite to perfection.

Flaubert in this describes the realm of the inauthentic, as one describes a circle; his novel marks out the limits of the given orders of language, where those limits are wide indeed. Only the work, this art, can stand outside the circle of stupidity, break free from the clinging common sense of Flaubert's nineteenth century; but it can do this only by representing that sense, by quoting and juxtaposing the given orders, moving across, around and through them. There is no outside except in impersonality or silence, the latter, as we saw, close to the former which, in turn, is the artist's version of silence; hence the need for strategies of silence in writing, for the eviction of meaning from the given meanings, including from the novel as expected social form, for the cancellation of its stability of representation.

Along with montage, there are further modes of draining meaning from the novel's world. The realisation of time, for example, involves a scale of temporalities that can be read in standard novel terms: instants of particular actions narrated as such, as in 'She quickly packed her bag, paid her bill [*fit sa malle, paya la note*]' (III,2); indications of the repetition through time of habitual doings, as in 'She ordered dishes for herself and left them untouched [*se commandait des plats pour elle, n'y touchait point*]' (I,9); passages of an imaginary time, Emma's projections of a different life, with imperfect and conditional tenses articulating these reverie–visions, giving them as immediate but unreal, as in 'they came to a fishing-village. . . It was there that they would live, in a low house with a flat roof in the shade of a palm tree [*ils arrivaient, un soir, dans un village de pêcheurs. . . C'est là qu'ils s'arrêteraient pour vivre; ils habiteraient une maison basse*]' (II,12). Yet this latter temporality is used to give an intensity of presence (with no transition, village and house are vividly before us) that already moves us away from any standard, is part of a fundamental disruption of the active historical time – meaningfully progressive and *effective* – to be found in a Balzac novel. Real time runs into imaginary time which becomes intensely present, takes over from the real time that is equally – indeed even more – vacant, one of stasis and degradation, as Emma goes to her inevitable end, as things rot away, as nothing changes.

Proust remarked that action in Flaubert becomes impression, and 'impression' is a word which appears in the early scenarios and sketches, along with 'sensation', 'atmosphere', and 'feeling', as Flaubert's reminder to himself of the effect to be achieved: 'inside of Rollet's [*sic*] house – filthiness – Léon's impression' (*NV*, 64); Sartre expressed irritation at the loss of action resulting from the novel's composition in tableaux, so many scenes – the ball, the inn on the first evening in Yonville, the agricultural show, and so on – that spread out the amorphous repetitive time of the provincial life; while Flaubert himself acknowledged his writing as lacking in events and worried that 'the reader will expect to see more movement': 'Still, one must do as one intended' (15 January 1853, C). What is striking is the reversal of the usual subordination of generalising habitual – 'iterative' – time to singular narrative-event time, and the way in which the former then comes to dominate our perception of the novel.

The tense of this is the imperfect, Flaubert's development of which, in conjunction with the shift it involves in the use of other tense and grammatical elements, was acclaimed by Proust as a renewal of our vision comparable to Kant's renewal, with his categories, of our theories of cognition and the reality of the external world. Flaubert's imperfect alters the aspect of people and things, modifies the boundaries of narrative and non-narrative, pulls background (as it would conventionally be seen) into the world of action and transposes action into the monotony of a continuum: a repetitive, futile senselessness of events and gestures. The imperfect, that is, becomes the very mode of narration, with narrative coming out more as description – the tableaux – than action. After the Vaubyessard ball, Flaubert has a chapter narrating Emma's life in Tostes until the departure for Yonville (I,9): a few small events are singularised, recorded in the preterite, the expected narrative tense – the visit from Emma's father, for instance; the bulk of the chapter, however, is in the Flaubertian imperfect, with singularity covered in tedium, just more of the same, making no difference. 'She wore [*Elle portait*] an open dressing-gown, that showed under the shawl-shaped collar a pleated blouse with three gold buttons': the detail suggests a particular occasion that the imperfect here negates, giving not a state at a specific time as background to some significant action but the action itself, since Emma's story *is* this iteration, this stasis of world and doings that nothing can alter. 'She listened [*Elle écoutait*] with dull attention to each stroke of the cracked bell': one Sunday and every Sunday are the same, quiescent in this imperfect. 'Then she went up again, shut the door, poked the fire and . . . felt boredom come down on her more heavily still [*Puis elle remontait, fermait la porte, étalait les charbons, et . . . sentait l'ennui plus lourd qui retombait sur elle*]'; the imperfect takes over narrative sequence, again equating singular and habitual in an overall monotony – 'the continuous tableau of a bourgeois existence' (15 January 1853, C).

What these individual instances can barely suggest is the cumulative effect of the use of the imperfect, both in this chapter and throughout the book. Emma, the chapter tells us, 'was waiting for some event', which comes – she gets pregnant, moves from Tostes – and never comes – what difference can such events make? The imperfect runs the vision of the book, is everywhere, and what that vision recognises as fate can then be grasped exactly as a temporality, rather than some destiny. There is no action, no escape, only recurrence, time at a standstill; change is merely the same again (Homais triumphs, more stupidity) or collapse and disintegration (of Emma's life and body). Events indeed, of the kind that Emma believes the ball to be, are gaps, rifts in the continuum, moments that can have no reality in time: 'The visit to La Vaubyessard had made a hole in her life' (I,8).

The attrition of action, the hollowing out of events, is carried on too through the symmetries, repeats, deflating echoes that are the very structure of the novel which includes everything, fatally and derisively, in a literal duplicity. Significantly, the word 'two', *deux*, occurs some 229 times (making it one of the most frequently used in the novel); everything is duplicated, done again. There are two balls (the one at La Vaubyessard, the masked ball in Rouen), two processions (at Emma's wedding, at her funeral), two prizes (Emma's at the convent, the old woman's at the agricultural show), two impossible conversations with the priest (Emma's, Homais's); Rodolphe's seductively soft boots come back as the varnished boot of the splendid new leg that Emma buys the luckless Hippolyte (Homais after all had promised him success with women); the powdered sugar that dazzles Emma with its whiteness at La Vaubyessard turns into the white powder of the arsenic she swallows at the end; the erotic vision of Emma at Les Bertaux, head back, 'the tip of her tongue slid between her exquisite teeth licking with little movements at the bottom of her glass' (I,3), reappears grotesquely as she dies, 'the whole of her tongue protruded from her mouth' (III,8). Nothing is distinct, meaningfully itself; repetition and symmetry are the reverse of any productive movement of differences, of any narrative sense; duplication brings only deprecation, degradation, decay. 'Her hair's undone, it looks like being tragic' (II,15), says Charles at the opera as Lucie enters for the mad scene, with Emma's frenzy – the deathbed scene of her convulsions – still to come. If the novel looks like being tragic too, Charles has here already undercut any such perception of it, making 'tragic' his word and view (he will respond to Emma's death with a whole 'voluptuousness of grief', following her to the grave as Edgar follows Lucie) –

and how can we see *with him*? Isn't it, if tragedy, the tragedy
of the absence of tragedy, of the lack of any significance?
Emma's death is nothing, insignificant; and not even untragic,
since we have no position to fix the novel as saying that either:
we *can* after all also see with Charles, there is no *better* view
in the novel, and this, characteristically, disables any one
decided reading, plunging us into an abyss – a hole – in
meaning.

Madame Bovary is full of holes, moments when the novel spirals
in on itself, pushing ironies of self-reference to a dizzying exhaustion of sense in its world. 'It would be impossible, surely, to see
a more perfect representation of nothingness', announces the
verger in Rouen cathedral to an impatient Léon and an irresolute
Emma, pointing to a sculpted figure 'about to descend into the
tomb' (III,1). His discourse – the litany of his guided tour – is
by rote, it means nothing; but then whose language is not by rote,
not just a mechanical repetition of words and phrases? At
another level, then, for the reader, the verger's discourse says
something even if it means nothing: it indicates something about
language – our orders of discourse – and it also gives a
premonition of what is to come, tells the truth of Emma at this
point, since she is likewise poised on the edge of the tomb. It does
more still, for it is equally applicable to the novel itself, '*Madame
Bovary*' as perfect representation of nothingness, perfect not just
for its creation of the figure of Emma, but for the very art of
Flaubert's work as well, its chiselled, balanced, firm-lined style.
Blind in his discourse (only the blind man escapes such blindness,
his discourse kept to a few snatches of song and the cry of his
putrid body), the verger nevertheless provides the reader with a
sight of the truth of the novel: it represents nothingness. But,
irony again, the novel too is included in that truth: after all, the
verger's sentence is just another platitude, as such a response to
the novel would be, indeed *as the novel itself may be* – '*Madame
Bovary*: perfect representation of nothingness'. The writing
spirals, turning the reader round and round again and then again.
Perfection, style, art are worth what? The cathedral spire is 'a
sort of truncated funnel, oblong cage, perforated chimney that

chances itself grotesquely on top of the cathedral like an essay in the extravagant by some fantastical tinker' (*ibid*). This is not the verger but a narrating voice: onto the story of Emma, Flaubert grafts — chances — the polish of sentences, the convolutions of style; is his novel the achievement of art or a tinker's fantasy, or aren't they one and the same? As Emma and Léon leave, the guide pursues them with 'a score or so of stout paper-bound volumes. . . works *dealing with the cathedral'*. What is the best-known work that deals with the cathedral? Answer: *Madame Bovary*. The novel falls in on itself, implodes: the ludicrous guide proffers the ludicrous book, where does the derision end?

Ink comes out of Emma's body, a stream of black liquid, Flaubert's essence; Charles's body is opened up and Canivet, the doctor, finds nothing. What else is there to find? Ink and emptiness, words and void. The novel continues to implode: Charles after all is just a character in a novel, a paper–ink–words being, nothing inside. Homais, thick in blood and sense, takes over, ends the novel. In a draft, in an explicit version of the turning-round against the novel suggested with the verger, Flaubert had him confront the novelist: 'aren't I just a character in a novel, the fruit of a delirious imagination, the invention of some nonentity whom I saw born and who invented me to make believe that I don't exist?' (*NV*, 129). Who is deriding who? The bourgeois is more powerful than the artist whom the bourgeois anyway invented, anyway set up and recognised and relegated as sentence-polisher — so Homais or tinker, who wins? The artist–craftsman who cast the cathedral's great bell 'died of joy' says the verger. Did Flaubert?

Some fantastical tinker, 'quelque chaudronnier fantaisiste'. Human speech is 'comme un chaudron fêlé', the cracked cauldron on which we beat out tunes to make a bear dance though striving to move the stars to pity. The tinker's fantasy and the everyday failures of language: Flaubert in *Madame Bovary* says both, which makes the novel *more*, a certain kind of consciousness, acutely poised in its specific unity, its specific poetic. Homais's rebellion does not come through into the final novel, we have only traces, the book turning itself inside out but then turning itself back again: reflexive and realist, ironic and pathetic, empty and full of meaning; with that balance, that indecision of its impersonality, making precisely its representation, its argument.

We come back to style and art, Flaubert's words for such a representation. As Sartre put it, 'Style is the silence of discourse, silence in discourse.' To aim at style is to aim at a disengagement from the noise of language in the world, all the viscous stupidity of its pronouncements; which is then to find some possibility of meaning, under and through and against words. Distance allows for closeness, moments of silence that can catch our sympathy for Emma or Charles. The 'absolute way of seeing things', Flaubert's definition of style, is to see things absolutely, suspending any discourse *on* them in the interests of the presentation *of* them, what Flaubert calls '*the illusion*', 'the first quality of Art' (16 September 1853, C).

Emotion can be obtained easily enough with melodramatic and sentimental effects, laying it on with some rhetoric of feeling. Art, on the other hand, seeks admiration as response, and its morality consists in its beauty: 'Style, form, the indefinable Beautiful *resulting from the conception itself* and which is the splendour of the True' (18 March 1857, LdC). The conception produces a beauty that is indefinable inasmuch as it is to do with making a work of art; there is no defining commitment outside of that making. The artist's duty is to art alone, and art exists solely in and for itself, something which 'always appears insurrectional to governments and immoral to the bourgeoisie (*OC* II, 761). Art must act − this is its supreme and most difficult achievement − 'in the manner of nature; that is, *making you dream*. . . the most beautiful works. . . are serene in appearance and incomprehensible. . . bottomless, infinite, multiple' (26 August 1853, C).

'Masterpieces are stupid [*bêtes*] . . . they have the tranquil look of the productions of nature' (27 June 1852, C), stupid in this very tranquillity, obstinately *there*, not because of some reaching-out with a conclusion, some laying down of a particular meaning. Prose 'must stand straight from one end to the other, like a wall', wrote Flaubert at the time of *Madame Bovary*

(2 July 1853, C), and the analogy of the wall was a significant one for him in this connection, relating to the violent pleasure he once experienced in front of a 'completely naked wall' of the Acropolis: 'I wonder if a book, independently of what it says, cannot produce the same effect' (3 April 1876, GS). If unity is everything, it is as the condition for the work of the achievement of this impregnable, inexorable reality, the realisation of an inner force of self-sufficient existence. Such a realism of the work matches the realism of the world: things are to be seen 'as they are' and the impersonal world can itself be considered as a work of art whose procedures the artist must respect and reproduce. Style does not change but transfigures the world for us, holds things to the vision − God-like, unified, reflective − it creates.

From his first literary aspirations through to *Bouvard et Pécuchet*, Flaubert was occupied with all the *bêtise* of his modern age, bent from the first on his role as demoraliser: 'I will only tell the truth but it will be horrible, cruel, naked' (24 February 1839, EC). *Madame Bovary* is a book written from that truth. But it is a book written too from Flaubert's desire, all the desire that at the same time it displaces, brings down to earth with its alien subject, alien yet close, and its wretched heroine, wretched yet close. It is this tension that gives the novel its force, its life, its style indeed, leaving the reader in movement, caught unresolvedly in the play of its demoralisation and its desire, its politics of language and its poetics of silence, the commonplace of pathos and the pathos of the commonplace; the reader held to this impersonality of writing, to work as wall and cracked cauldron, statement in and as itself of all 'the eternal, lamentable and serious irony of existence' (9 June 1852, C).

Chapter 3

Madame Bovary: sequels and effects

'I'm fed up with *Bovary*. They wear me out with it'
(16 February 1879, Georges Charpentier)

Late in his life, Flaubert would insist that he never wanted to
hear of *Madame Bovary* again: 'the name alone annoys me'
(13 June 1879, RdG). This disaffection, we saw, was part of
its very writing as a book undertaken against the grain of
Flaubert's desire: 'don't judge me on it. . .it was a matter of
set purpose, an exercise in composition' (30 October 1856,
RdG). Exasperatingly, his first published novel, cut off from
his natural lyricism ('everything I like isn't in it', *ibid*), achieved
a notoriety that fixed him as *its* author, just 'Flaubert, author
of *Madame Bovary*'. And this even as his work continued, as
the other novels were published: *Salammbô* (1862), the purple
novel of war and passion in the Carthage of antiquity, begun
soon after *Madame Bovary*; the second *Education sentimentale* (1869), using the career of its (anti-) hero in Paris in the
1840s and 50s to grasp the historical reality of contemporary
society; and those two great extreme projects that sum up his
raison d'écrire: *La Tentation de saint Antoine* (1874), the book
of the unleashing of the imagination through saintly ascesis,
and *Bouvard et Pécuchet* (1881), the posthumous novel of the
two clerks who set out to explore human knowledge from
geology to literature, agriculture to theology, and who end up
back at a desk copying, like Flaubert himself, the compiler of
this commonplace book, lost – impersonal – in all the
stupidity of the human. Since his death, each of these novels
has, in fact, been singled out as centrally – and often
exclusively – important: for James, for Sartre, Flaubert was
Madame Bovary; for Proust, for Kafka, he was supremely
L'Education sentimentale; for Valéry, who not unlike Flaubert

himself detested *Madame Bovary* and 'its "truth" of reconstituted mediocrity', the significant book was *La Tentation*; for Barthes and others in recent years, it has been *Bouvard et Pécuchet*; and mention must also be made again of the *Correspondance* which has itself been treated as a major book, a great portrait–novel–document of the modern writer. Yet *Madame Bovary* remains the generally known and pre-eminently influential work: through its cultural reverberations, through its definition of the novel, through the vicissitudes of its readings and re-readings across the years.

The Goncourts called *Madame Bovary* 'the last word of the true'. Impersonality, interest in the given facts of existence, reproduction of everyday life, absence of the novelistic (no elaborate plot, no striking events, no exceptional characters), these were the features recognised in Flaubert's novel, making it the key reference for the next generation of realists and the development of naturalism. In England, the stir caused by the trial led to a certain immediate awareness of the novel and determined hostile reactions to its shocking realism. Only much later was the book made available in English, in the transla-tion by Marx's daughter Eleanor published in 1886 by Vizetelly and Co. Vizetelly was himself brought to trial in 1888 for publishing translations of Zola, and while *Madame Bovary* was not mentioned at the trial, it was part of the general indict-ment, another example of the kind of literature at which the prosecution was aimed. The dominant English response, indeed, throughout the century, was very much one of disgust at immorality and recoil from the book's perceived cold-bloodedness, what Matthew Arnold in 1887 called 'the cruelty of petrified feeling'. The same recoil was to continue, enshrined in the influential 'great tradition' of the novel as moral form established by the critic F. R. Leavis in the 1940s, from which perspective Flaubert and *Madame Bovary* could represent only an immature cynicism, a failing in 'intensity of moral preoc-cupation'. Leavis, in fact, merely echoed Lawrence, a vital figure in his great tradition: 'all the modern stuff since Flaubert' has no tragic power inasmuch as it is merely acceptance and resignation, delivers no 'great kick at misery' — 'I hate it.'

This will already have suggested something of the continuing presence of Flaubert's novel, the way in which it stood and stands as necessary point of reference and reaction. The type of the naturalist novel for Zola, it equally prompted other defining appropriations, the history of the novel then including dialogue with *Madame Bovary* as one of its significant factors: the rewriting, more or less critically, of the terms of its presentation of contemporary reality and, in particular, of woman. Lawrence's own novels were no exceptions, and *The Rainbow* (1915) and *Women in Love* (1921) need especially to be understood in the argument they engage with Emma's story. Before Lawrence, and itself indeed contributing importantly to his argument, the major English example of rewriting was the work of Hardy, above all *The Return of the Native* (1878) whose heroine, Eustacia Vye, is carried away by the strength of an idea of love derived from her romantic reading: 'To be loved to madness — such was her great desire.' Hardy's involvement was perhaps mediated via Elizabeth Braddon's *The Doctor's Wife* (1864), which may be the earliest borrowing from Flaubert's novel in English, though Braddon omits adultery and is given to moralising. These English examples, moreover, are part of a much wider European response and can be paralleled in the novels of other literatures, most notably in *Anna Karenina* (1877) which, as George Steiner has put it, 'embodies Tolstoy's close experience and partial denial of the presentation and moral judgement of adultery in *Madame Bovary*'. Flaubert's novel became a general cultural fact, an inevitable reference. What else would Dostoevsky's Nastasya Filippovna in *The Idiot* (1869) be reading just before her attempted suicide? What else would the young Sartre do in a letter to his mistress but assure her of his wish that she should have 'an attitude of mind that in the midst of the most mediocre existence will stop your life from being a failure, you from being a Madame Bovary'? Which brings us further than realism and the historical importance of *Madame Bovary* as realist novel, brings us to Madame Bovary and the historical importance of her portrayal.

The figure of Emma gave expression to a psychological state that it crystallised; catching up a modern fact of feeling and behaviour, it provided the very type for that fact and was from then on its definitive representation. Hence *bovarysme*, the term and the concept derived from *Madame Bovary*, the perception that the novel brings into being. The word itself was perhaps coined by Barbey d'Aurevilly who used it in 1862 in a review of a now forgotten novel, describing the heroine as lapsing into uninhibited sensuality and corruption, 'into a state of absolute *bovarisme* [*sic*]', but the crucial systematic account was proposed by the philosopher Jules Gaultier in two works at the end of the century: *Le Bovarysme: la psychologie dans l'œuvre de Flaubert* (1892) and *Le Bovarysme* (1902). For Gaultier, *bovarysme* was *the faculty of conceiving oneself as other than one is* and as such represented an evolutionarily valuable human possibility. This depends, however, on the stimulation of a *higher* conception of oneself, an aspiration for the better. When the goal aimed at is unobtainable, mere fantasy, *bovarysme* is damaging and ultimately pathological. It is this pejorative sense of the term Gaultier finally stressed and that became current, unsurprisingly given its derivation from Flaubert's novel and the conventional condemnations of Emma. *Bovarysme* appeared in psychiatric textbooks as a disorder of the imagination; involving profound disgust at reality, dissatisfaction with one's life, flight into imagined worlds, and resulting in a neurotic − specifically hysterical − state. It also entered language more generally − in English sometimes anglicised as 'bovarism' − to express what the *Oxford English Dictionary* defines as '(domination by) a romantic or unreal conception of oneself'; or what T. S. Eliot in 1927 characterised as 'the human will to see things as they are not'.

The focus on Flaubert's novel as the definition of a psychological condition and an exemplary case history was fundamental to its influence. *Madame Bovary*, in the middle of the century, condensed and expressed a new conception of the feminine, of woman. *Bovarysme* is gender neutral, a condition affecting both sexes, but at the same time above all a matter of women, of Madame Bovary in this − *her* − drama of hysteria. What is woman, what does she want, what is her identity? In the figure of Emma, Flaubert finds terms for the crisis around women and the idea of 'the woman', produces a representation of the new social reality of the tensions and contradictions in women's situation. Concomitantly, he participates in the development of an understanding of sexuality that extends the idea of the sexual beyond some mere assumption of 'the sexual act' with fixed identities of 'man' and 'woman'; an assumption that was Marx's, for example, even as his daughter was working on her translation of *Madame Bovary* − and translating it too in her own life, living through something of what Emma represents, herself brought, in a painful repetition, to suicide by poison. The society's oppressiveness, all the bourgeois order of things, is stated by Flaubert through the oppression of this woman; since 'the woman' is a prime ideological investment of that order, of its truth, and since women as such are then exactly marginal by virtue of their emblematic centrality, their non-existence other than as that image of 'the woman', other than in the Homaisian discourse of angels and whores, mothers and hysterics. The entry for 'woman' in the *Dictionnaire des idées reçues* reads: 'Person of the sex   What is appropriate for a woman   Current importance of woman   Do not say "*ma femme*" but "my spouse", or better still "my better half"   One of Adam's ribs' (*BP*, 516). The woman stands for sexual−social order; women must be held to the appropriateness of 'woman', to 'the sex' as propriety; and this is now an *issue*, there is a need to reinforce and enforce the required terms of identity as man and woman, the one and the other, she as his complementary half, Adam's rib indeed. Behind those terms lies disorder, trouble, the scandal she also represents and increasingly threatens, her hysteria ('to be confused with nymphomania', *BP*, 529).

Flaubert's artistic critique, his struggle for art against the bourgeois world, thus finds its analogue in sexual critique, in the challenge women can pose to that same world. Before Charcot, before Freud, at the beginning of all the medical−psychological work around 'the woman question', Flaubert already, decisively, forces the issue, moves hysteria from sickness and pathology to critique and writing − his writing of Emma. *Madame Bovary* should be read in close conjunction with John Stuart Mill's *The Subjection of Women* (1869) and Freud's *Studies on Hysteria* (1895), three texts by men which mark the latter half of the nineteenth century with a fundamental recognition of something askew, opaque to the established fictions of understanding, outside and in contradiction of the given sexual–social economy. When Freud records his surprise that his scientific papers read like novels, we can see that it is not so surprising, that what he is doing is to take up the understanding that had already been produced in literature, *Madame Bovary* above all. Thus there is no question of converting *bovarysme* into some feminine *essence*; on the contrary, the novel proposes it through Emma as a great representation of women in their situation in the nineteenth century, outrageously shattering the current social conventions. The psychology of Emma is women's and the novelist's clinical demonstration of the society of Homais; *bovarysme* and hysteria are critique as well as symptom, and it is on the grounds of their critical possibility that Flaubert – the hysteric Flaubert, himself self-confessed as a chronic case of *bovarysme* – encounters and develops Emma. Their encounter initiates a line of successive accounts, rewritings of Emma, which are so many explorations of the social–sexual through a central heroine whose depiction provides a dissenting focus on the existing reality and whose creation is dependent on, extends and transforms that original, initiating figure: Ibsen's Hedda Gabler in his play of that title (1890) and Kate Chopin's Edna Pontellier in *The Awakening* (1899) are obvious examples (both these heroines come, differently, to suicide).

Bovarysme itself could be taken up as an assertion against the male world, as a kind of utopian poetry for women consciously espoused for difference and change. George Egerton in her *Keynotes* (1893) proposes a heroine who 'fancies herself in Arabia on the back of a swift steed. Flashing eyes set in dark faces surround her, and she can see the clouds of sand swirl, and feel the swing under her of his rushing stride. Her thoughts shape themselves into a wild song, a song to her steed of flowing mane and satin skin; an uncouth rhythmical jingle with a

feverish beat; a song to the untamed spirit that dwells in her.'
The line from the young Flaubert through Emma is evident
(orientalism included, with all its race fantasies of 'the other'),
but Egerton revalues what Flaubert finally distanced in Emma;
the heroine's thoughts here shape themselves into romance,
wild song, and there is no gap between thoughts and writing
(no free indirect style) to break their authentic power. So many
other women may have 'this thirst for excitement, for change,
this restless craving for sun and love and motion', and so many
of them will remain unknown or known only through 'stray
words, half confidences, glimpses through soul-chinks of suppressed fires, actual outbreaks, domestic catastrophes' – which
closely returns us to Flaubert's depiction of Emma, and brings
us too to its literary historical importance for male writers.
What Flaubert suggests in his encounter with Emma is the
possibility of a position 'as a woman' – Nietzsche's hated
'feminisation' – that becomes powerful as an imagination and
a strategy of writing for the modern male artist: to write outside, against the given terms of reality and identity, *is* to write
'feminine', since woman is outside and against, a disturbance
to those terms. Joyce ends *Ulysses* (1922) – another novel of
adultery, another scandal, another legal battle – with the
monologue of Molly Bloom, just as he ends *Finnegans Wake*
(1939) with the flow of Anna Livia: the feminine projected not
as the last word, but as the elision of all those last words from
the accepted orders of discourse into a writing in process, free-
ing from the fixed reality.

The realism of *Madame Bovary* and the achievement through
its heroine of a decisive social–sexual representation do not ex-
haust its influence. Decisive too was Flaubert's commitment
to making his novel a work of style and art. Epitome of realism,
Madame Bovary was also influential as the conversion of the
novel to literary value. *Madame Bovary* was taken as a beginning of what James called 'the art of fiction', and the critic
Percy Lubbock appealed to it as the 'novel of all novels' in
his significantly titled treatise *The Craft of Fiction* (1921),
which itself drew heavily on James and his development of that

Flaubertian art. James, who read *Madame Bovary* in early youth and had some personal acquaintance with its author, saw faults in the novel, failings in Flaubert's vision of the human, remained unhappy with the 'poverty' of Emma's consciousness which he considered too limited to be the focalising perspective (his own *The Portrait of a Lady*, 1881, is, explicitly, yet another rewriting of Flaubert's novel). None of this, however, prevented his recognition of it as 'rare in its kind': 'perfect to this point, nothing else particularly matters'. The perfection is that of form: 'The form is in *itself* as interesting, as active, as much of the essence of the subject as the idea, and yet so close is its fit and so inseparable its life that we catch it at no moment on any errand of its own. . . The work is a classic because the thing, such as it is, is ideally *done*, and because it shows that in such doing eternal beauty may dwell' (the Flaubert of the aims set out in the *Correspondance* could hardly have found a better reader). This interest of the form in itself, the perfection with which the work is 'done', is precisely what makes Flaubert the novelist's novelist and *Madame Bovary* his masterpiece: the inescapable exemplar of the craft of fiction, the major reference for any poetics of the novel.

It was taken as exemplary also of the necessity of art, of the need for the strength of style. For Ezra Pound, concerned in the early years of the twentieth century with the revitalisation of English writing in the face of the 'blurry' sentimental vagueness of a conventional Victorian literature, Flaubert indicated a precision that is 'the ONE sole morality of writing': '[he has done] a great deal of the real or fundamental brain work for nearly all good narrative writers since his time'. Pound's major example of such a writer in English learning from Flaubert's 'hard clarity' of style was Joyce – '[he] has taken up the art of writing where Flaubert left it' – and Joyce indeed cited Flaubert as one of the three or four writers whose every line he had read. Flaubert's famous statement on the artist in his work as being 'like God in the universe, everywhere present and nowhere visible' was translated by Joyce into the similarly famous description, in the last chapter of *A Portrait of the Artist as a Young Man*, of the artist as remaining, God-like, 'within or behind or beyond or above his handiwork, invisible, refined out of existence, indifferent, paring his finger-nails'. As Flaubertian artist, Joyce also knew the obsession with 'the perfect order of words in the sentence', the devotion to style: as he put it to his brother Stanislas, in words that are in essence Flaubert's, 'I'm not interested in politics. I'm only interested in style.'

Such a stance reflects that idea of the modern artist's commitment to art so powerfully exemplified by Flaubert's dedication to the writing of *Madame Bovary*. 'I am nothing but literature', declared Kafka who constantly compared himself with Flaubert; Proust, for whom Flaubert stood as the example of the realisation that the artist's life is in art alone, with everything else 'an illusion to be described', retired into his cork-lined room; Joyce went into literal exile; all live literature after Flaubert as difficult and exclusive calling. It is with him that literature becomes *essentially* problematic, neither sustainable as universal (there is a new awareness of class and history, of the social reality of language and meaning), nor reducible to its commerce (there is an alienation from class and history, from this society, in the very name of a universality nevertheless, the imagination of an ideal − art − against the particular social values and sense). The writer is thus either commercial agent, meeting the demands of the mass culture, or self-conscious artist, split between the necessity of writing and its impossibility − what can it mean to write in this world with this language? To which the answer is art, writing in opposition to industrial literature and its world, outside its parameters of production and consumption. But then − the contradiction − still within them, produced in and eventually valued for its very art by the society from which it seeks to separate.

In the face of that society, the writer − aiming as artist at perfection and beauty − must of necessity be demoraliser, ironist, farcical moralist, constantly and critically pressing on its limits, disengaging from the available languages. The im-personality sought by Flaubert, as by Joyce in his wake, is not that of some confident objective grasp of a truth, but that of the disappearance of any such confidence, the elision of the writer — and so of the reader — into the play of the languages that make up the world, leaving only the intransitive work, with its objective truth of art alone. *Madame Bovary* and *Ulysses*, poised in their hesitation of any position, ironic and lyric, then give way to *Bouvard et Pécuchet* and *Finnegans Wake*, the finally impossible texts, books in which nothing can be told except the interminable writing of the silence that can never come from under the thickness of sense: all the versions of knowledge Flaubert copies out; that can never come from under the babel of language: all the 'sinse' over which Joyce mulls in his gigantic comedy of words and letters and sounds. Which leaves Beckett — the third of these 'stoic comedians', as Hugh Kenner has called them — with the task of grinding writing to silence in 'senseless, speechless, issueless misery': 'Having nothing to say, no words but the words of others, I have to speak. No one compels me to, there is no one, it's an accident, a fact.' We are far from, but nevertheless at one end of, *Madame Bovary*: the book about nothing Flaubert envisaged while writing his novel, trapped in this consciousness of 'no words but the words of others', which the latter anticipates in theme (decay, emptiness, nothingness) and form (impersonality), is realised in Beckett's novels as the stutterings of an 'I' emptying itself in the production of a discursive void: no meaning, only the fading of the successive, repeated words, and the contingence of a very few — less and less — insignificant objects, just stubbornly things.

What Beckett explicitly remembers from *Madame Bovary*, in *Molloy* (1951), is the description of Charles's cap (I,1), referred to in Moran's son's school-cap and again in the hat of the man who comes to Moran's shelter: 'The hat was quite extraordinary in shape and colour. I shall not attempt to describe it.' Charles's cap becomes the prime example of what Robbe-Grillet calls 'improbable objects as regards the economy of meaning'; objects which are silent, gratuitous, for which no sense is made in story or discourse (where a Balzac saturates objects with narrative significance and social meaning, declares their sense to the reader). *Madame Bovary*, concludes Robbe-Grillet, is 'a *nouveau roman* before its time': Flaubert initiates a subversion of the novel — of the genre of the bourgeois appropriation of the world, of the expression of its coherent 'reality' — that the new novel, the *nouveau roman*, continues. The realist Flaubert undermines realism, points to resistance of object and fact of sentence, problematises story and reading. Robbe-Grillet extends the green silk cigar-case dreamt over by Emma after the Vaubyessard ball into a metaphor for the modern novelist: 'the coloured silk threads going from hole to hole, intertwining their continually broken paths so as to form the pattern. Isn't that precisely the metaphor for the work of the modern novelist (Flaubert is me!) on the weave of the real, full of gaps, writing and then reading going from lack to lack in order to build up the narrative?' The real begins where meaning wavers, and it is such an effect that the writer today seeks to produce: writing as an undermining of existing representations which, grasped as such, form the material for his or her novel or *text* ('novel' suggests complicity with the old illusions of representation). The modernity of Flaubert is that from *Madame Bovary* onwards, he wrote in and wrote out that situation of literature and the writer.

From realism and naturalism to modernism and the new novel, example and source for a Zola, a Joyce, a Robbe-Grillet . . . What can be seen in this diversity of response is the continuing power of Flaubert's novel, its existence as a site of constant questioning, for an unceasing activity of appropriation and reappropriation. *L'Idiot de la famille*, Sartre's huge treatise, is simply the most monumental tribute to this power, *Madame Bovary* taken as the great expressive work of our current history, raising all the contemporary questions of writing, reality and subjectivity. Aiming at the creation of a literary object, the novel as self-contained work, a unity of art through style, Flaubert made a book, a text, that states, articulates, represents the modern problematic of inauthenticity within which writer as well as character are involved, Flaubert and Emma both — how, again, is one to write, and what is one to write, and what credit is to be given to reality, its representation, one's language? Inheritor and harbinger, Flaubert takes the romantic artist into modernist consciousness: the artist is a hero doomed to disappear, condemned to ironisation or silence, to exile in the tortures of style and the asceticism of art, to knowledge of the fictions of discourse and the materiality of language. *Madame Bovary* is 'permanent' (Pound's favourite word for Flaubert's work): permanent in its place in the history of the novel (realism, psychologisation of novel and character), in the history of consciousness (the figure of Emma, *bovarysme*, hysteria and the feminine), in its modernity (the new practice of writing). Unlike any other novel that went before, it developed techniques (impersonal narration, *style indirect libre*, montage-juxtaposition) and modes of vision (inauthenticity as the new substance of reality; human as object, object over human; a temporality of movement in stasis; an idea of art and the artist's calling) that have given it an influence few novels can equal.

'How can it be doubted that Flaubert is the precursor?', wrote *nouveau romancier* Nathalie Sarraute in 1965. It cannot indeed. But then the specificity of Flaubert's novel must not be doubted either, its permanence too as this particular work with all its density: the weight of its own reality and the reality to which it responds, against which it pushes. *Madame Bovary* is a novel of the 1850s by a writer of the 1850s. Modern today, modern in its time, *Madame Bovary* does also give a mid-nineteenth century realism its devastating ultimate definition, crystallises a moment of history in its radical attempt through art to deal with a world that was loathed but impassable, in a form — the novel — that was inimical but inevitable, round a figure — Emma — who was distant but close, and who became a paradigm figure of modern experience, just as the author-artist — Flaubert — did himself. *Madame Bovary*, Emma Bovary, Flaubert — this is the achievement, they together making up this landmark of literature.

Guide to further reading

Works by Flaubert and material relating to *Madame Bovary*

The best available French edition of *Madame Bovary* is that by
Claudine Gothot-Mersch cited in the Note on references, but the novel
is also easily and adequately available in several paperback collections
(e.g. Collection Folio, Paris, Gallimard, 1972). The Textes et Con-
textes edition, Paris, Magnard, 1988, provides the text of the novel
together with a large selection of extracts from historical documents
and critical essays, making it an invaluable resource for the student.
Madame Bovary, Nouvelle version précédée des scénarios inédits,
edited by Jean Pommier and Gabrielle Leleu, again cited in the Note
on references, prints initial plans, scenarios and sketches, as well as
giving a new continuous text of the novel obtained by amalgamating
its final version with discarded draft material. Bibliographical details
of the most useful current edition of Flaubert's complete works and
of the editions for his letters are also given in the Note on references.
His other novels can easily be found singly in various paperback
editions (Folio, Flammarion GF, Le Livre de Poche).

There have been a number of English translations of *Madame Bovary*
since that by Eleanor Marx-Aveling published in 1886. Those most
readily available are:

Gerard Hopkins (1949), Oxford, Oxford University Press (World's
    Classics), 1981.
Alan Russell (1950), Harmondsworth, Penguin Books (Penguin
    Classics), 1950.
Lowell Blair (1959), New York, Bantam Books (Bantam Classics),
    1981.
Mildred Marmur (1964), New York, New American Library (Signet
    Classics), 1964.
Paul de Man (1965; a 'substantially new translation based on the
    version by Eleanor Marx-Aveling'), New York and London,
    W. W. Norton and Co. (Norton Critical Editions), 1965.

None of these is satisfactory (Flaubert himself apparently oversaw

a translation by one of his niece's English governesses — 'a masterpiece', 12 June 1862, EF — but it has never come to light): the Norton version often maintains a certain helpful closeness to Flaubert's
writing procedures (it also includes translations of a number of
scenarios and drafts as well as of some important critical documents
— notably the reviews by Sainte-Beuve and Baudelaire); the Penguin
Classics version is often preferable to that of the World's Classics;
the Signet Classics version is often more stylish than its Bantam
Classics United States rival (the latter, like the Norton, though less
substantially, adds a dossier of extracts from criticism of the novel,
notably from the crucial essays by Zola and Maupassant, together with
a short selection from Flaubert's letters). Translations of Flaubert's
other major works can be found in the Penguin Classics series.

Transcripts of the prosecution and defence speeches at the trial, as
also of the court's judgement, were included by Flaubert in the 'Edition
définitive' of *Madame Bovary* published by Charpentier in 1873; these
can be found in the Intégrale *Œuvres complètes* (*OC* II, 724–50). An
English version of this material, trans. Evelyn Gendel, is included in
the Signet Classics *Madame Bovary* listed above. Dominick LaCapra's
Madame Bovary on Trial, Ithaca and London, Cornell University
Press, 1982, provides an excellent account of the trial and the questions of reading posed by the novel.

The *Mémoires de Madame Ludovica*, owned and perhaps commis-
sioned by Flaubert, can be found in Douglas Silier ed., *Flaubert et
Louise Pradier: le texte intégral des 'Mémoires de Madame Ludovica'*,
Archives des lettres modernes (145), 1973.

Biography

Though not entirely reliable, Maxime Du Camp's *Souvenirs littéraires*,
2 volumes, Paris, Hachette, 1882–3, contain numerous biographical
details concerning Flaubert, together with invaluable first-hand
accounts of the context, publication and trial of *Madame Bovary*
(relevant sections are included in *OC* I, 19–37). Edmond and Jules
de Goncourt's *Journal* (written over the period 1851–96), 3 volumes,
Paris, Laffont, 1989, is full of insights and anecdotes concerning
Flaubert and offers a unique impression of the literary and artistic
world he frequented (the comment on the prosecution of *Madame
Bovary* as an attack on romanticism comes in the entry for 20 January
1857, I, p. 232; the description of Flaubert's novel as the ultimate
word of truth in that for 10 December 1860, I, p. 642). The most recent
biography is Herbert Lottman, *Gustave Flaubert*, London, Methuen,
1989; marred by occasional inaccuracies and a certain naivety, it never-

theless offers a useful and detailed account of Flaubert's life. Julian Barnes in his best-selling *Flaubert's Parrot*, London, Jonathan Cape, 1984 tells a great deal about Flaubert and gets something of the feel of him in a small number of readable pages. The unsurpassable account of Flaubert and his life up to and including the writing of *Madame Bovary*, however, is the Pléiade *Correspondance*, with its comprehensive editorial notes by Jean Bruneau – extraordinary letters in a magnificent edition.

Jean-Paul Sartre explores the relation of Gustave to *Madame Bovary* – how does this individual become the author of this book? – in a gigantic work of understanding that, although at odds in places with the biographical evidence and prone to repetition, is one of the most powerful accounts ever of the making of a writer and his/her text: *L'Idiot de la famille*, first published in 1971–2, but now available in a new revised edition with additional material: 3 volumes, Paris, Gallimard, 1988 (volume III of this edition contains the fascinating notes Sartre made towards the unwritten fourth volume, which would have consisted of a detailed analysis of *Madame Bovary*); quotations here are from I, p. 1081 (Gustave defining himself through desire), II, p. 1626 (style as silence), III, p. 772 (Emma as lacking Jules's conclusion in art). A translation is underway: by Carol Cosman, *The Family Idiot*, 3 volumes published so far, Chicago, University of Chicago Press, 1981, 1987 and 1989 (translation volumes do not correspond to French ones; at the close of its third volume, the translation is nearing the end of the second volume of the French). For a helpful introduction to Sartre's study, see Hazel Barnes, *Sartre and Flaubert*, Chicago, Chicago University Press, 1981. Reference should also be made to Sartre's *Questions de méthode*, Paris, Gallimard, 1960; trans. Hazel Barnes, *The Problem of Method*, London, Methuen, 1964; chapter 3 contains a short discussion of what is at stake in grasping Flaubert in terms of the relations of existential project and historical situation (beginning from that recognition of Flaubert as the father of realism but feminine).

For classic accounts of Flaubert's early writings and the genesis of *Madame Bovary*, see:

Bruneau, Jean, *Les Débuts littéraires de Gustave Flaubert, 1831–1845*, Paris, Armand Colin, 1962.
Gothot-Mersch, Claudine, *La Genèse de 'Madame Bovary'*, Paris, José Corti, 1966.

Reference should also be made to Jean-Yves Mollier's *Michel & Calmann Lévy, ou la naissance de l'édition moderne 1836–1891*, Paris, Calmann-Lévy, 1984, which gives much information about Flaubert's dealings with his publisher, as, more generally, about developments in publishing in nineteenth-century France.

Critical works

Key 'historic' essays are:

Sainte-Beuve, Charles-Augustin, '*Madame Bovary*' (1857), *Causeries du lundi*, XIII, Paris, Garnier, 1858, pp. 283–97.

Baudelaire, Charles, '*Madame Bovary*' (1857), *Œuvres complètes*, II, Paris, Gallimard, Bibliothèque de la Pléiade, 1976, pp. 76–86; translation included in *Madame Bovary*, Norton Critical Editions, pp. 336–43.

Zola, Emile, 'Gustave Flaubert' (1875/80), *Les Romanciers naturalistes* (1881), Henri Mitterand ed., *Œuvres complètes*, Paris, Cercle du livre précieux, 10, 1968, pp. 97–155.

Maupassant, Guy de, 'Gustave Flaubert', preface to *Lettres de Gustave Flaubert à George Sand*, Paris, Charpentier, 1884 pp. i–lxxxvi.

James, Henry, 'Gustave Flaubert' (1893) and 'Gustave Flaubert' (1902), in Morris Shapira, ed., *Henry James, Selected Literary Criticism*, Cambridge, Cambridge University Press, 1981, pp. 138–54, 212–39.

Proust, Marcel, 'A ajouter à Flaubert' (1910) and 'A propos du "style" de Flaubert' (1920), *Contre Sainte-Beuve*, Paris, Gallimard, Bibliothèque de la Pléiade, 1971, pp. 299–302 and 586–600; trans. John Sturrock, *Against Sainte-Beuve*, Harmondsworth, Penguin Classics, 1988, pp. 89–91 and 261–74.

There have been a large number of more modern critical studies, from discussions of specific aspects of *Madame Bovary* to more general accounts of the novel, as well as of its relations to Flaubert's work as a whole. Particularly significant here are:

Auerbach, Erich, *Mimesis: The Representation of Reality in Western Literature* (1946), trans. Willard Trask, Princeton, Princeton University Press, 1953.

Brombert, Victor, *The Novels of Flaubert* (1966), second revised edn., Princeton, Princeton University Press, 1968.

Colloque Flaubert (Rouen, 1969), *Europe*, September-October-November 1969, 3–278 (see especially: Claude Duchet, 'Roman et objets: l'exemple de *Madame Bovary*', 172–201).

Culler, Jonathan, *Flaubert: The Uses of Uncertainty* (1974), revised edn., Ithaca, Cornell University Press, 1985.

Genette, Gérard, 'Silences de Flaubert', *Figures*, Paris, Seuil, 1966, pp. 223–43.

Girard, René, *Mensonge romantique et vérité romanesque*, Paris, Bernard Grasset, 1961; trans. Y. Freccero, *Deceit, Desire and the Novel*, Baltimore, Johns Hopkins University Press, 1965.

Gothot-Mersch, Claudine, ed., *La Production du sens chez Flaubert* (Colloque de Cerisy-la-Salle 1974), Paris, Union Générale des Editions, 1975.

Kenner, Hugh, *Flaubert, Joyce and Beckett: The Stoic Comedians*, Boston, Beacon Press, 1962.

Knight, Diana, *Flaubert's Characters: The Language of Illusion*, Cambridge, Cambridge University Press, 1985.

Picard, Michel, 'La prodigalité d'Emma Bovary', *Littérature*, 10, May 1973, 77–97.

Poulet, Georges, 'Flaubert' (1949), *Etudes sur le temps humain*, I, Paris, Union Générale des Editions, 1972, pp. 346–63; trans. Elliott Coleman, *Studies in Human Time*, Baltimore, Johns Hopkins University Press, 1956, pp. 248–62.
'Flaubert', *Les Métamorphoses du cercle*, Paris, Plon, 1961, pp. 371–93; trans. Carley Dawson and Elliott Coleman, *The Metamorphoses of the Circle*, Baltimore, Johns Hopkins University Press, 1966, pp. 249–65.

Prendergast, Christopher, *The Order of Mimesis*, Cambridge, Cambridge University Press, 1986.

Robert, Marthe, *En Haine du roman: étude sur Flaubert*, Paris, Balland, 1982.

Rousset, Jean, 'Madame Bovary ou le livre sur rien', *Forme et signification*, Paris, José Corti, 1962, pp. 109–33; translation of this chapter on *Madame Bovary* included in *Madame Bovary*, Norton Critical Editions, pp. 439–57.

Schor, Naomi, 'Pour une thématique restreinte: écriture, parole et différence dans *Madame Bovary*', *Littérature*, 22, May 1976, 30–46; 'For a Restricted Thematics: Writing, Speech, and Difference in *Madame Bovary*' in Schor, *Breaking the Chain: Women, Theory and French Realist Fiction*, New York, Columbia University Press, 1985, pp. 3–28.

Sherrington, R.J., *Three Novels by Flaubert: A Study of Techniques*, Oxford, Clarendon Press, 1970.

Tanner, Tony, *Adultery in the Novel*, Baltimore, Johns Hopkins University Press, 1979.

Vargas Llosa, Mario, *La Orgía perpetua: Flaubert y Madame Bovary*, Madrid, Taurus, 1975; trans. Helen Lane, *The Perpetual Orgy*, London, Faber, 1987.

Ullmann, Stephen, 'Reported Speech and Internal Monologue in Flaubert' (1957), *Style in the French Novel*, Oxford, Basil Blackwell, 1964, pp. 94–120.

Other references

Mademoiselle Leroyer de Chantepie's letters to Flaubert are included in the Pléiade *Correspondance*; for her initial response to his scalpel-like analysis of provincial life and the situation of women there, see her letter of 18 December 1856. The letter by George Sand setting out her wish that Flaubert had made the moral lesson of *Madame Bovary* more obvious and objecting to the inhumanity of impartiality can be found in Alphonse Jacobs ed., *Correspondance Flaubert–Sand*, Paris, Flammarion, 1981: 12 January 1876. Note that the Pléiade *Correspondance* also includes her letters to Flaubert to the end of 1868. For Amélie Bosquet's report of 'Madame Bovary, c'est moi', see René Descharmes, *Flaubert, sa vie, son caractère et ses idées avant 1857*, Paris, Librairie des Amateurs, 1909, p.103 n.3.

The medical dictionary referred to in the discussion of hysteria is the *Dictionnaire des sciences médicales*, 60 volumes, Paris, C. L. F. Pancoucke, 1812–22; the entry for hysteria is in volume XXIII, 1818, pp. 226–72. The *Traité clinique et thérapeutique de l'hystérie* by Dr Pierre Briquet was published in Paris by J. B. Baillère in 1859; arsenic is envisaged as a cure on p. 706. Jean-Martin Charcot's insistence on the laws of hysteria is cited by Georges Didi-Huberman in his account of Charcot's work in the Salpêtrière hospital in the last decades of the nineteenth century: *Invention de l'hystérie*, Paris, Macula, 1982, p. 78.

Louise Colet's keepsake story 'Qui est-elle?' is in *Le Royal Keepsake*, Paris, Mme Vve Louis Janet, 1842, pp. 120–41. The vaudeville farce mocking Madame Bovary opened on 12 December 1857 at the Théâtre du Palais-Royal and was published the following year (by Flaubert's publisher!): A.-C. Delacour and P. A. Lambert-Thiboust, *Les Vaches landaises*, Paris, Michel Lévy, 1858 (the snatch of Emma's song is on p. 40). Jules Gaultier gave *bovarysme* its psychologico-philosophical development in *Le Bovarysme: la psychologie dans l'œuvre de Flaubert*, which appeared monthly in the *Revue de la France moderne* from April to August 1892, and, more substantially, in *Le Bovarysme*, Paris, Mercure de France, 1902. T. S. Eliot defined the term in 'Shakespeare and the stoicism of Seneca' (1927), *Selected Essays*, London, Faber, 1952, p. 131. Barbey d'Aurevilly used *bovarisme* in his review of *Antoine Quérard* by Charles Bataille and Ernest Rasetti in *Le Pays*, 11 August 1862; reprinted in his *Les Romanciers* (*Les Œuvres et les hommes*, IV), Paris, Amyot, 1865 (see p. 290). His review of *Madame Bovary* was in *Le Pays*, 6 October 1857; reprinted in *Les Romanciers*, pp.61–76. Its discussion by Armand de Pontmartin comes in his 'Le roman bourgeois et le roman démocrate: MM. Edmond

About et Gustave Flaubert', *Le Correspondant*, 25 June 1857; quotations here are from pp. 290 (democracy in the novel), 300 (equalisation of people and things) and 303 (the novel as photographic apparatus). The second edition of Ernest Feydeau's *Fanny*, Paris, Amyot, 1858, has the preface by Jules Janin in which he makes the comments on realism (p. ix) and on moral requirements in the presentation of adultery (pp. xiii–xiv). For Champfleury on realism, see his *Le Réalisme*, Paris, Michel Lévy, 1857 (tired of versified lies, p. 5; shunning schools like cholera, p. 36); his direct response to Flaubert and his novel is recorded in letters written in 1856–7 to fellow-novelist Max Buchon and published in 1919 in *La Revue Mondiale*, 1 December (see p. 541) and 15 December (see p. 702). Duranty's statements on realism come from the first number of his journal *Le Réalisme*, 15 November 1856, pp. 1–2; his remarks on *Madame Bovary* were made in a brief review in the fifth number, 15 March 1857, p. 79. Louis Ulbach remembers the time of the publication of Flaubert's novel by the *Revue de Paris* in *Misères et grandeurs littéraires*, Paris, Calmann Lévy, 1885 (the passage describing his initial reading of it is on pp. 2–3). Sainte-Beuve analyses the democratic invasion of literature in 'De la littérature industrielle' (1839), *Portraits contemporains*, I, Paris, Didier, 1852 (the actual phrase appears on p. 502).

Les Français peints par eux-mêmes, encyclopédie morale du dix-neuvième siècle was published in 9 volumes by L. Curmer, Paris, 1840–2; including Frédéric Soulié, 'L'âme méconnue' (I), Hippolyte Lucas, 'La Femme adultère' (III), and Honorée de Balzac, 'La Femme de province' (VI). Pierre Joseph Proudhon's insistence on adultery as the all-embracing crime can be found in his *De la Justice dans la Révolution et dans l'Eglise* (1858), in *Œuvres complètes*, IV, Paris, Marcel Rivière, 1935, p. 307 (reading the book, Flaubert was indignant at Proudhon's literary opinions – 'What a brute!', 27 January 1859, EF – though he took one of its aphorisms on women, 'Woman is the despair of the just man', to be 'the thought of a Genius, quite simply', 11 January 1859, EF). For *L'Amour* (1858) and *La Femme* (1859), see Paul Viallaneix ed., Jules Michelet, *Œuvres complètes*, XVIII, Paris, Flammarion, 1985; quotations are from pp. 42, the century of the womb, and 178, woman as the illness (Flaubert was scathing: on the first, 'It's the apotheosis of marriage, the idealisation of the conjugal fart, the delirium of home cooking', 27 January 1859, EF; on the second, 'What a fool old Michelet is! He seems to me to be jealous of Balzac who got further than him into the moral and physical privates of the sex I worship', 4 December 1859, Aglaé Sabatier).

For Nietzsche's attitude to Flaubert and his novel, see particularly

The Case of Wagner (1888), trans. Walter Kaufmann, in Kaufmann ed., *Basic Writings of Nietzsche*, New York, Random House, 1968. The 1830–50 comment, made in the 1880s, is in *The Will to Power*, ed. and trans. Kaufmann, New York, Random House, 1968, p. 66. D. H. Lawrence made his comment on *Madame Bovary* lacking any 'kick at misery' in a 1912 letter; *The Letters of D. H. Lawrence*, I, ed. James T. Boulton, Cambridge, Cambridge University Press, 1979 (p. 459); his complaint at Flaubert's withdrawal from life is in 'German Books: Thomas Mann' (1913), *Phoenix*, London, Heineman, 1961 (p. 312). F. R. Leavis supports Lawrence's criticism in his *D. H. Lawrence: Novelist* (1955), Harmondsworth, Penguin, 1964, pp. 25–7; see too his initial devaluation of Flaubert for weakness of moral preoccupation in *The Great Tradition* (1948), Harmondsworth, Penguin, 1962, pp. 40–2. Paul Valéry's dislike of *Madame Bovary* is recorded in his essay 'La Tentation de (Saint) Flaubert' (1942), *Œuvres*, I, Paris, Gallimard, Bibliothèque de la Pléiade, 1968, pp. 613–19. Georg Lukács's idea of the 'dual critique' was quoted from *The Meaning of Contemporary Realism* (1957), trans. John and Necke Mander, London, Merlin Press, 1963 (p. 61). Ezra Pound stresses the importance of Flaubert's precision and of Joyce's response to it in numerous pieces in the 1910s and 1920s, collected in Forrest Read, *Pound/Joyce*, London, Faber, 1968. Vladimir Nabokov sees *Madame Bovary* as a prose poem in a lecture dating from the 1940s, *Lectures on Literature*, London, Weidenfeld and Nicolson, 1980, p. 171. Alain Robbe-Grillet's remarks on Flaubert's modernism are to be found in *Le Miroir qui revient*, Paris, Minuit, 1985, pp. 208–21; trans. Jo Levy, *Ghosts in the Mirror*, London, John Calder, 1988, pp. 146–53. Nathalie Sarraute's recognition of Flaubert as determining modern literary presence is elaborated in 'Flaubert le précurseur', *Preuves*, February 1965, pp. 3–11; trans. Maria Jolas, *Partisan Review*, Spring, 1966, pp. 193–208. Roland Barthes discusses Flaubert and the problematisation of literature in *Le Degré zéro de l'écriture*, Paris, Seuil, 1953, pp. 47–8; trans. Annette Lavers, *Writing Degree Zero*, London, Cape, 1967, pp. 69–71. Matthew Arnold's 'Count Leo Tolstoi' (1887) is in R. H. Saper ed., *The Complete Prose Works of Matthew Arnold*, XI, Ann Arbor, University of Michigan Press, 1977, with the criticism of *Madame Bovary*'s petrified feeling on pp. 292–3. The comment by George Steiner on *Madame Bovary* and *Anna Karenina* was taken from *After Babel*, Oxford University Press, 1975 (p. 456), which also includes a brief illuminating discussion of the problems of translations of Flaubert's novel (pp. 372–7). For George Egerton's romance rewriting, see *Keynotes* (1893), London, Virago, 1983, pp. 19 and 21. *Molloy* by Samuel Beckett appeared in French in 1951 and then in an English version in 1955; the extraordinary hats can be found on pp. 119 and 134 in *The Beckett Trilogy* edition, London, Picador,

1979. Sartre's 1926 letter was quoted from *Lettres au Castor*, I, Paris, Gallimard, 1983 (p. 20).

Finally, reference to the statistical improbability of Emma's suicide was based on Christian Baudelot and Roger Establet, *Durkheim et le suicide*, Paris, Presses Universitaires de France, 1984.